Jointly published by:

AFRICAN PUBLISHING GROUP (INTERNATIONAL)
P O Box BW 350, Harare
ZIMBABWE
&
NGORONGORO CONSERVATION AREA AUTHORITY
P O Box 1, Ngorongoro
TANZANIA

First published 1999, Second Edition 2000

© David Martin. Pictures as credited, maps and published edition APG, 1998
ISBN: 1-77901-140-7
Photographic credits. All David Martin except pages 6, 24, 42, 55, 56 (main picture), 58/59, 80 and 83 (NCAA/Reinhard Kunkel), and pages, 19, 28, 31 and 33 (John Reader)
Design: Paul Wade, Ink Spots, Harare
Origination: Creda Communications, Johannesburg
Printing: Creda Communications, Johannesburg

CONTENTS

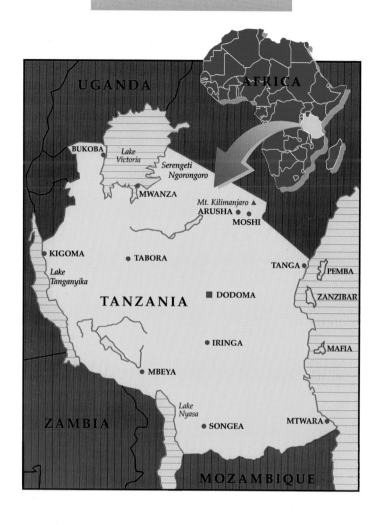

Acknowledgements

I am especially indebted to the Conservator of Ngorongoro Conservation Area, Emmanuel Chausi, the Chief Manager (Tourism), Paul Mshanga and the Assistant Conservator (Tourism Development), Steve Lelo, for their knowledge and support in the preparation of this guide. Further valued support was given from the authority by the Senior Ecologist, Victor Runyoro, Saning'o Ole Telele, the Extension Officer of the Community Development Department, and Benjamin Margwe, Damian Massay and Israel Naman, all of the Tourism Department.

Tanzania National Parks provided transport and for their support I am grateful to the Director Parks Management and Conservation, Gerald Bigurube, the Public Relations Manager, James Lembeli and my driver, Augostinho Pasia. Finally I am grateful to Lota Melamari of TANAPA whose vision triggered this Tanzanian series and whose encouragement, despite personal adversity, sustained it.

Ngorongoro Serena Safari Lodge provided the accommodation for the bulk of my work and I must particularly thank Wanjohi Githaiga, Engelbert Mkindi and their staff. Last, but not least, Hugh McCullum in Harare rough edited the early drafts and Judy Boyd and my colleague and companion, Phyllis Johnson, fine-tuned it and encouraged me throughout.

This book is the second in a series of at least seven area-specific guides to Tanzania. *Serengeti: Endless Plains* is already published. Forthcoming are *Kilimanjaro: Africa's Beacon*, *Zanzibar: Spice Islands*, *Tanzania's Northern Circuit*, *Tanzania's Southern Circuit*, and *Coastal Tanzania*.

These are "travel guides with a difference" as *Africa Travel News* put it. The visitor is treated as a discerning person and not fed the usual diet of adjectives and pretty pictures without substance. To begin with, they are introduced to an area and its geology, environment, history and people. Then the mammals, birds, trees and shrubs are detailed. The guides end with details about facilities, where to stay, checklists, further reading and an index. Finally, the guides accompany the visitors on the trip home, and thus remain a visual and accessible memory of a remarkable journey.

David Martin
Ngorongoro.

INTRODUCTION

Ngorongoro's first conservator, Henry Fosbrooke, described the crater as the world's "Eighth Wonder" while, somewhat more sparingly, German conservationist, Professor Bernard Grzimek, described it as "...one of the Wonders of the World".

Such descriptions, particularly in reference to the crater alone, may be regarded as excessive by custodians of "wonders" not listed among the seven ancient ones of the world. That list, which few can remember beyond schooldays, is limited to Middle East human construction.

Beauty — and wonders — are very much in the eye of the beholder. No doubt Fosbrooke and Grzimek, whose association with Ngorongoro jointly spanned over 60 years, would have ranked it number one, for this was their backyard.

Ngorongoro Conservation Area

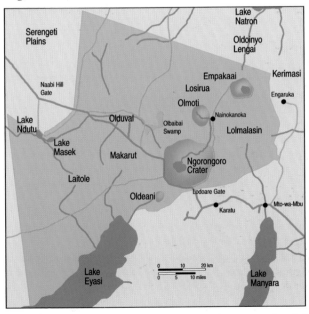

Opposite page: A heavily tusked elephant set against the crater wall and clouds

More accurate, however, is the description of German Professor Wilhelm Kattwinkel, the first foreigner known to have stumbled on Olduvai Gorge, part of Ngorongoro Conservation Area. Olduvai, he later wrote, contains the "...book of life".

Ngorongoro vital statistics

The Ngorongoro Conservation Area is 8292 sq km varying in altitude from 1020 m to 3587 m. The terrain embraces several quite distinct habitats from open grasslands to mountain forest and from scrub bushland to highland heath.

The centrepiece of Ngorongoro is in fact a caldera — the largest unflooded and unbroken one in the world — and not a crater as it is usually called. A caldera has a diameter many times the size of the vent through which a volcano once spewed forth its debris of ash over the surrounding countryside. The caldera is formed by the inward collapse of the volcano.

Ngorongoro Crater is 19.2 km in diameter, 610 m deep and 304 sq km in area. The floor of the caldera is 261 sq km and this area contains a small soda lake and abounds with wildlife ranging from the largest carnivores (meat eaters) to the smallest herbivores (plant eaters).

Ngorongoro lies in northern Tanzania in what was once volcanic terrain. To the east is the Gregory Rift Valley, source of the salt lakes of Manyara and Natron, famous for their pink flamingo, and Africa's highest peak, Mount Kilimanjaro. Only one volcano, Oldoinyo Lengai (Maasai for the Mountain of God), is still occasionally active.

To the west of Ngorongoro are the endless, open grassland plains of the Serengeti bounded in the south and north respectively by the Eyasi Rift Scarp and the Oldoinyoogol Hills where the Rift Valley is still visible. The semi-arid wastes of the Eyasi Rift Valley lie to the southwest and to the north. The flat, dusty plain of Salei crosses into neigbouring Kenya while increasingly, modern agriculture is seen on the southeastern slopes of the volcanic range.

For most people, whether they have arrived by air or overland, the 165 km journey to Ngorongoro begins at the northern Tanzanian town of Arusha, a bustling and congested provincial capital where numerically the potholes in the roads compete with tour operators and safari vehicles.

Arusha conjures up memories of an old-style Wild West town in its early days. Mount Meru, Tanzania's second highest mountain, which can be snow-capped in winter, looms over the frontier town where the old and the new compete for space and attention.

Home of the Wa-Arusha, who are related to the Maasai, and Wa-Meru people, the town's population density exceeds 1500 per sq km compared to an average of only 75 for the 945087 sq km country. Banana and coffee plots and plantations ring the town while churches, bars and hotels are dwarfed by a sprawling office and conference centre in the middle of the town which is located midway between the Cape and Cairo.

The visitor senses the population's tough and indomitable pioneer spirit and determination. Ox-drawn carts, carrying water in discarded oil drums, demand equal space on the roads with modern limousines. Curio sellers and other vendors clutter the roadsides and pavements and virtually everywhere there are self-described *fundis* (Swahili for experts) for everything from cars to computers.

The one that got away

From Arusha, the visitor travels west, leaving the town past large coffee plantations, a Greek church, and the busy light aeroplane airport. The lushness of the Arusha area gives way to eroded, undulating countryside pock-marked with distinctive hills. Nomadic Maasai linger, the children, with hands proffered, seeking money. It is unwise to photograph them without permission and payment.

The road from Arusha to Makuyuni, which leads to the Tarangire National Park and the country's political capital, Dodoma, is tarmac and takes about an hour. Self-drive visitors should beware of the unmarked speed humps.

At Makuyuni, which contains little more than a petrol station, a basic restaurant, a few shops and some curio sellers, the road to Ngorongoro turns right and now the safari really begins.

A black-maned lion asleep; his massive paws and legs are used to stun prey

Apart from the Gregory Rift in the distance, this part of the journey is more memorable for the road than scenery and Mto-wa-Mbu village, which means "mosquito creek" in Swahili, provides a welcome break in the journey. Its marketplace is worth a visit.

From Mto-wa-Mbu you climb the rift with magnificent views over Lake Manyara, through parched countryside in the dry season, passing several hotels and colourful curio shops, before entering the fertile agricultural country inhabited by the Mbulu who are more correctly called the Iraqw.

Tsetse kept the Maasai out of this area until the 1920s while two world wars played a part in the area being unoccupied. The country, known as Tanganyika (it united with Zanzibar in 1964 and became Tanzania) re-emerged after Germany's defeat in the First World War as a British trust territory. Previously it had been called German East Africa.

During the war, German-owned property was seized and then sold by the British Custodian of Enemy Property. When the ban was lifted on German residence in the 1920s, those Germans who subsequently settled had to find somewhere new to live.

Mto-wa-Mbu

The inhabitants of Mto-wa-Mbu are a heterogenous group who, like true pioneers, have in the past 75 years carved out a niche for themselves in this largely inhospitable landscape.

Water drew them to the site and it is the lushness of their surroundings, with a tumbling river providing the source for irrigated cultivation and a plentiful crop of citrus fruits and vegetables, which provides the first insight into the importance of Ngorongoro and the rift.

The area is dependent upon the forests of the Ngorongoro highlands for its water supply. There are few natural springs; rain water is absorbed by the porous volcanic soils and forest mulch and roots, with the water appearing again as gushing springs and rivers at the foot of the rift. One such river is crossed just past Mto-wa-Mbu opposite the entrance to Manyara National Park.

They chose the lower slopes of Oldeani, an inactive volcano south of Ngorongoro, and began carving out coffee farms from the bush and forest.

The remains of the Seidentopf house (above) and part of a pre-First World War plough (inset) provide a reminder that the Germans once farmed part of the crater

These farms needed labour and it was this that drew the Iraqw people, first as labourers and later as smallholder-settlers in their own right. A 1940s British Government report recommended that unalienated land south of the boundary of the Northern Highlands Forest Reserve be developed for the Iraqw.

The pace of development quickened after the Second World War during which the German settlers in the area were once again removed to British concentration camps.

Karatu became the trade centre of this area and, together with Oldeani and Mbulumbulu, between Karatu and Ngorongoro, proved particularly suitable for wheat. The Custodian of Enemy Property, who was running the former German farms on behalf of Britain, had established an official wartime wheat scheme for the area which included ploughing the Iraqw lands on a short-term lease. The land was to be handed back at the end of the war.

Disputes arose when the time came to return the land. It belonged to the Iraqw people and agricultural technology had long existed in the area as evidenced by the usage of canals and terraced irrigation. But the white commercial farmers and contractors possessed the know-how and money to grow wheat — and they owned the machinery.

A compromise was finally reached pooling resources and sharing profits. From their share of the profits the Iraqw people bought their own machinery, becoming increasingly self-sufficient and expanding the acreage under cultivation. Government interference and investment was minimal with local common sense being the driving force, making the Mbulu resettlement scheme a model.

From the Karatu area, the visitor climbs through the Ngorongoro Lodoare entry gate into temperate evergreen forest, a mix of tall trees and evergreen shrub, over a dirt all-weather road which is much better than the section traversed from Makuyuni.

Now beckon the vast caldera, the highlands and the Serengeti beyond. But it is worth reflecting that much of what you have seen on the journey — at the busy village at Mto-wa-Mbu, in the forests, at the river and lake at Manyara, and in the fields of wheat, maize, bean and coffee around Mbulu — derive their lifeblood from the rains at Ngorongoro which are absorbed and recycled to be used by those you will have seen on your journey.

Tanzanians say "karibu" in Swahili, meaning welcome, the greeting you are likely to receive here

GEOLOGY

Ngorongoro Crater has only existed in its present form for two to three million years which, given the fact that the planet is over 4000 million years old, geologically makes it a comparatively young wonder.

A very long time ago, sea covered the Ngorongoro area. Mud and sand were then deposited on the ocean floor by ancient rivers. As the floor sagged under the increasing weight, more and more debris was heaped on top. The bottom layers compacted under the weight. Sandstones, mudstones and shale were formed and the temperature rose.

Below, from the earth's core, molten lava began to invade the space being taken by the newly formed rock. The additional heat, combined with the new chemical elements introduced by the molten material, speeded up the process of change.

The molten lava forced its way through faults in the newly formed rock mantle and gradually the molten rock cooled and solidified as granite. During cooling it became brittle and the earth's crust created by the outer rock layer was subjected to violent movements.

Geologists are not sure when this occurred. Certainly it was at least 500 million years ago and, on the basis of evidence from elsewhere in Africa, it may have occurred 1000 and possibly 2000 million years ago.

The rocks, which had been moulded in the depths of the former ocean trough, rose to the surface to form land masses, and the oceans retreated. Without protective vegetation, which was only to develop later, the newly formed land mass was exposed to the daily heating and cooling of the sun. Rain, without soil cover to absorb it, pounded the rock faces in a slow destructive phase which today is known as erosion.

About 400 million years ago plant life began to cover the rocky land surface. With it, soil developed and the rocky mass grew a protective cover. Erosion remained the constant force, gradually whittling away

Opposite page: The different colours of this environment-moulded and weathered hill at Olduvai reveals the differing geological ages

the earth's surface and exposing the ancient crystalline rocks which lay beneath. Whole hills were worn away and replaced by gently undulating plains with the first features of today's topography beginning to emerge.

Birth of the Rift

Two hundred million years ago the super-continent, Pangaea, started splitting, creating the beginning of the continents as we know them today. About 70 million years ago the outline of the African continent was drawn and had taken the position it now occupies. Fifteen to 20 million years ago this long period of erosion came to an end with the massive and perpetual movement in the earth's core tearing a fracture through much of Africa from the Red Sea to the Kalahari in Namibia. This resulted in the 6400 km long African or Great Rift Valley.

The land to the west and northwest of Ngorongoro marked the fracture line which cut through the Oldoinyoogol Hills and along the western shore of what is now Lake Eyasi where towering 300 m high cliffs still mark the rift. The main part of the hills were on the elevated platform left by the upheaval, while the foothills were on the lower platform, which subsided between 1000 and 2000 m.

Geologists refer to such fracturing and rock displacement as a fault. When an area is cut into distinct blocks, such as the elevated block at Loirujruj in the extreme southwest, this is called rift-faulting. The steep cliffs encountered at Manyara and elsewhere are known as fault or rift scarps.

This faulting, which divided the area into two visibly distinct parts, also heralded the onset of volcanic activity. Initially this was confined to the east of the rift and molten lava was thought to have reached the surface through the fractures opened up by faulting.

These lavas, called flood basalts by geologists, were very fluid, capable of travelling long distances before solidifying. They literally flooded the lower altitude plains of the rift running from Oldoinyoogol and Eyasi, spreading as far east as where Kilimanjaro is located today.

Late in the flood basalt phase, vents, instead of elongated cracks or faults, provided the molten lava's escape to the surface. Seven such vents are known to have existed in the area now known as the Crater Highlands, and the lava released from these accumulated around them instead of flowing across the landscape. On these vents sites Ngorongoro's seven volcanoes, each growing to over 4000 m in height, established themselves.

Ngorongoro five to seven million years ago

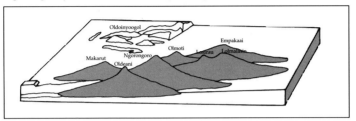

This string of volcanoes included Ngorongoro, Oldeani, Makarut, Olmoti, Losirau, Lolmalasin and Empakaai and the volcanic debris spewing from them blew westwards covering today's southern Serengeti Plains.

There are 20 major volcanic centres in the region including Mount Kilimanjaro. The region is pockmarked with thousands of cones and craters, which places this area among the finest volcanic viewing scenery in the world.

Volcanoes, mighty as they may seem superficially, are mere pinpricks or orifices in the earth's crust through which gases and other matter are released from time to time. Like icebergs, the bulk of a volcano is hidden from sight. But icebergs reveal one-tenth of themselves, whereas what you see of a volcano is only a hundredth or even a thousandth part.

At its full height Ngorongoro probably reached at least 4587 m, 1308 m less than Kilimanjaro. But, unlike Kilimanjaro, Ngorongoro was subjected to a vast explosive eruption which blew away its top as well as part of the west side of Oldeani, forming the breached crater.

The building of this volcanic range was followed by secondary faulting, mainly to the east of the Ngorongoro Highlands, which produced the

Gregory Rift Wall. Once again the area to the east of the rift subsided. It was during this period that the Ngorongoro caldera as you see it today was formed.

Ngorongoro one to two million years ago

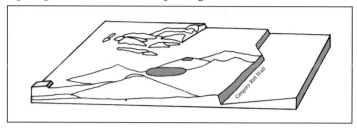

The highlands were subjected to a momentous upheaval with a large circular fracture developing around Ngorongoro. As a result the whole centre of the Ngorongoro volcano collapsed forming the caldera. Similar, but smaller, circular fractures occurred at Olmoti and Empakaai creating the calderas which exist today.

The sequence leading to the chain reaction which creates calderas is provoked by the withdrawal of the molten lava which previously existed below the volcano. Thereafter, volcanoes simply collapse into themselves.

In this period, the region's main drainage system came into existence. Lakes Manyara and Natron were formed at the base of the Gregory Rift with basins at Engaruka and Olmkoko between the two lakes.

Basins were created in the highlands at Ngorongoro, Malanja, Bulbul and Empakaai, while the Olmoti Crater formed a separate drainage centre.

These lakes do not have outlets to the sea because the onward passage of water is blocked by the surrounding terrain, or prevented during the dry season from overflowing.

As a result there is no escape for the minerals washed down with the water. These minerals simply build up in the lakes making the water alkaline and leaving soda pans on their shores, and when they dry up, this is good for the salt-makers.

The period in which the Gregory Rift and Ngorongoro caldera were created marked the peak of the region's seismic upheaval. Comparatively minor activity continued to the west and in the Ngorongoro area itself, and small knoll-like hillocks were formed. This phase of small-scale faulting happened about 150000 years ago and with a few notable exceptions the region's topographical map had been drawn.

The exceptions were Kerimasi and Oldoinyo Lengai just to the east of the Gregory Rift on its northern face. Prodigious quantities of lime-rich ash were produced by a series of eruptions at Kerimasi, and this ash was spread over a very wide area hardening to form grey or fawn limestone rocks.

Early human inhabitants in the area later used stone tools such as these

The ash reached as far afield as the western part of Ngorongoro. More significantly, the ash covered the Salei area, Olduvai Gorge and the Serengeti plains, further flattening the landscape. At the foot of the Oldoinyoogol range an ash cover more than 122 m thick was left.

While Kerimasi slid towards extinction, a new volcano, Oldoinyo Lengai, was being born only 11 km north. This volcano in turn threw up large quantities of black ash which again reached out across much of the area and can be found at Olduvai thereby assisting in precise dating of fossil remains. The ash also created a series of sand dunes to the west on the nearby plains.

Today Oldoinyo Lengai, which last erupted in 1983, remains the area's only active volcano.

The wildlife you will see at Ngorongoro and elsewhere is determined, in varying degrees, by four different factors affecting their lives — food, security, shade and water. In that they are not much different from human beings.

But humans can make their own food, police their own security, build their own shelter, and determine where their water is sourced and received. Animals cannot. They must meet their needs according to local circumstances and thus the habitat is the determining factor as to where a particular species is found.

Crinum Macowanii known as a pyjama lily

In this, Ngorongoro combines the best of all worlds for the wildlife — and for the visitor. But to fully appreciate the wildlife one must also try to understand the nature of the environment including the geology, soils, grasses, flowers, shrubs, trees and rains upon which they thrive.

A forest reserve lies in a band around the outer slopes of the eastern and southern extremities of the conservation area. Roughly it runs from Empakaai in the north to Oldeani in the south with a green finger of trees reaching in to the centre to embrace Olmoti.

Once through the Lodoare Gate you enter this moist and mountainous, high montane forest where, at some times of the year, mist and rain almost obscure the all-weather dirt road and moss-covered trees which overhang the road leave large puddles.

The forest reserve covers 890 sq km and it is an important botanical and wildlife sanctuary supporting a wide diversity of flora and fauna. It is also the catchment area for the wheat, maize and coffee fields you will have passed through in Karatu district.

The volcanic soils of the area do not vary greatly although the prevailing winds have dictated their shape and intensity. The major variation is in the rainfall pattern and this is what mainly determines the flora and fauna the visitor will see and upon which the species depend.

Abutilon Mauritianum

The rains

Ngorongoro, in common with most of East Africa, receives two distinct and independent periods of rain a year, the short rains in November and December and the long, and usually more intense, rains from March to May.

These rains are dependent upon two Indian Ocean monsoons which carry inland moisture-bearing clouds which are broken up by the high ground they encounter. The short rains tend to come from the northeast while the long rains come from the southeast.

As these rain clouds make their way from the sea they must first pass the Usambara Mountains west of the port of Tanga, then the Pare Mountains south of Moshi, and finally Kilimanjaro and Meru. On that journey they lose much of their moisture before reaching Ngorongoro.

At Ngorongoro, the bulk of the rain falls on the eastern and southern slopes, nurturing the forest reserve, interspersed with grassy clearings, which in turn provide the catchment area for Mbulu. In contrast, the western side of Ngorongoro receives comparatively little moisture and the area is described as being in a "rain shadow".

This rainfall-dictated pattern is repeated in miniature elsewhere in the area. While the eastern face of Oldeani is covered with an almost unbroken canopy of evergreen, only bamboo grows on the western side of the mountain.

The eastern rim and inner walls of Ngorongoro Crater are forested while the western rim and inner walls are grasslands with some shrubs and are generally devoid of evergreen forest. The area around the lodges and camp sites where the visitor will stay is a mixture of these two-worlds-in-one, but there is an absence of cedar here.

Cheetah

The reasons for this is apparent in the early morning. Etched against the sky and the volcanic background, moist clouds tumble over the eastern lip of the crater, dissipating before they reach the bottom. In contrast, the view to the west reveals the arid nature of the terrain in that direction which is only broken by a few rock outcrops known as *kopjes,* and Olduvai Gorge.

So in the first instance, what you are witnessing has been determined over millions of years by the earth's violent upheavals, the geological framework this left, the erosion of the landscape, the altitude and the resulting in rainfall patterns.

Into this mini-ecosystem various living things have moved, each having its localised niche.

Elephants, apart from their obvious need for security, require food and shade which they find in the forests, and water which they usually take once a day. Except when going for water, they are most likely to be found in the forests which offer both food and shade.

On the drive from Lodoare Gate to the lodges and camps the visitor is likely to see the prodigious droppings showing where elephants have passed. Less obvious are the indentations which elephants make by digging with their feet and tusks for mineral salts.

Buffalo require grassy areas such as those found on the crater floor and in forest glades. Around lodges and camp sites they can be very dangerous, which is why they are one of the most feared animals in the bush.

Rhinoceros, and prides of lion will be seen regularly on the crater floor. But cheetah, except when hunting, are much less conspicuous as are leopard whose larders in the trees may well be seen before they are.

Wildebeest, zebra and gazelle who participate in the migration, prefer the open grasslands which offer greater security from the ever-lurking predators. The side-striped, black-backed, and golden jackal as well as spotted hyena are all to be seen close to the herbivores.

> ### Lerai elephants
>
> *In the Lerai (the Maasai word for the yellow fever trees found in the area) Forest on the southern edge of the Ngorongoro Crater floor, large-tusked elephants, and the impact they have wrought upon the remaining trees, are evident. The number in the Lerai Forest is only around 30 and they are all solitary males. This is possibly because of the nutritonal content of their forage with females in calf needing a higher protein intake. However, larger numbers of elephants, including females and calves, exist in the forest reserve.*

Eland, the largest antelopes in Africa which weigh about 1000 kg, are to be found in and around the Lerai Forest, while hippopotamus, which can weigh two tonnes and move very quickly on land, are most commonly seen submerged in the Mandusi Swamp. Defessa waterbuck also live on the fringes of the Lerai Forest while the shy Bohor reedbuck may be seen around the Gorigor Swamp.

Several species such as giraffe, are absent from the crater floor. Giraffe can descend the crater walls but they are browsers which eat large quantities of the shoots of acacia trees and prefer umbrella acacia *(Acacia tortilis)*, whistling thorn *(Acacia mellifera)* and *Acacia seyal* not found on the crater floor. Other mammal species absent from the crater, but which appear on the Serengeti plains, include impala, topi and oryx.

Mammal numbers

There is a myth that the animals the visitor will see in the crater are confined to that area. This is not true. They do — as the migrating species illustrate — come and go. A total of 115 species of mammals have been recorded in the conservation area. Of these, 50 were on the crater floor which, for some, meets all their needs. Rhinoceros are one example with the crater floor offering greater security and making the population one of the largest surviving in the wild in East Africa.

Just how many animals there are in the conservation area is uncertain as the task of counting them accurately is made impossible by the forest cover. Those on the crater floor are thought to number around 25000 making Ngorongoro Crater the most intensive game-viewing area on earth.

But this figure can fluctuate according to the rains. The herbivores depend upon the availability of grass for food. When there is not sufficient they move on. The predators depend upon the herbivores for their food. Thus when the herbivores move on so must some of the carnivores.

Poaching is frequently given as the determining factor for the number of animals in the conservation area. But with the exception of commercial poaching for rhinoceros horns and elephant tusks, there is no evidence that poaching has impacted adversely on the animal population.

Rather, timber poaching — for firewood, building poles and cooking — on the forest fringe, settlements, the blocking of migration routes by cultivation, as well as disease, malnutrition, reproductive failure and the availability of food would appear to have combined to limit the wildlife population.

Wildebeest on the crater floor

Equally, the cover and terrain determines the birds, butterflies and other insects, as well as the reptiles which inhabit it. Some birds, usually less distinguishable and referred to as LBJs (little brown jobs), are seedeaters usually found in the grasslands.

Others eat fruit and prefer the forest cover while some, such as vultures, are scavengers feeding on the predators' kills. Another group, such as flamingos, are waterbirds found feeding and standing in, or on, land adjoining water such as Lake Magadi in Ngorongoro Crater.

Certain species of butterflies, moths, other insects and reptiles are restricted to the forest. Some species of butterflies, often determined by sex, fly higher in the forests with the females nearer the ground and thus more likely to be seen than the males. Some camouflage themselves with toxic repellents to protect against predators.

Everything has its reason for living where it does and behaving as it does. The habitat dictates the resident species habits and in this the rains are the key factor.

EVOLUTION: OLDUVAI

The importance of the archaeological finds at Olduvai, and the link they have provided in tracing the earliest history of humans, has tended to overshadow the equally important contribution the area has made towards understanding the evolving fauna and topography.

Olduvai contains evidence of the age of mammal gigantism. In those days there were sheep-like beasts with horns over six feet from tip to tip. Pigs had three-foot-long tusks and were the size of hippopotamus, while rhinoceros were twice the size they are today.

There was also an elephant called *Dinotherium.* It was one of the five original families of elephants and their ancestry can be traced back to a small pig-like creature known as *Moeritherium* whose fossil remains have been found in Egypt. *Dinotherium,* the Olduvai Gorge finds reveal, coexisted with the earliest human toolmakers.

Dinotherium had short downward curving tusks projecting from the lower jaw while today's elephants have upward curving tusks from the top jaw.

One of the 7000 worldwide extinct species unearthed at Olduvai was *Hipparion,* a three-toed horse.

> ### Olduvai Gorge
>
> *Olduvai Gorge is a deep erosion scar on the eastern edge of the Serengeti ecosystem. It runs from Lake Ndutu on the boundary between the Ngorongoro Conservation Area and the Serengeti National Park to the Olbalbal swamp and depression just west of Ngorongoro Crater.*
>
> *The gorge is about 50 km long, and at its deepest, close to where the main archaeological sites, visitor viewing platform and museum are located, it is about 70 m deep. To the north of this, the gorge becomes shallower.*
>
> *The correct name is in fact Oldupai, the more normally used word being a Europeanisation. In the Maasai language, Oldupai is the name of the wild sisal plant you will see in the area. Throughout this guide the more normally internationally known name, Olduvai, is used.*

Opposite page: The 3.75-million-year-old Laitole footprints. Note the footprints of a three-toed horse on the right

Much of this archaeological evidence is contained at the site museum where the evolution of the species, many with unearthed fossils, can be traced layer by layer in the unfolding story. It is well worth a visit with one of the resident guides, although one is left wishing that Tanzania would do more to maintain and publicise this unique attraction.

Confronting one of these massive mammals, by chance or when hunting, must have been intimidating for early humans who were comparatively puny in size and poorly equipped to defend themselves.

Laitole footprints

These footprints revealed that three hominids (early ancestors of humans), probably two adults and a child, had walked upright across the terrain some 3.75 million years earlier.

The Laitole discovery, which greatly pre-dated the earliest known occasion humans walked upright, was as important and exciting as parents watching their child rising from all fours to take its first tentative steps. The Laitole area is not accessible but imprints of the finds can be seen in the Olduvai museum.

The hominids who crossed the grey, desolate landscape at Laitole were much shorter than we are today, measuring only 1.2 to 1.4 metres when upright, and their brain size was less than 30 percent of ours. Their features were more ape-like with a prominent forehead above an angled face leading to pouted and protruding lips.

The ash from the volcanoes to the west laid down a unique filing system of these early events throughout the region and the framework for understanding our own origins.

Through the potassium argon technique it is possible to date accurately deposits of volcanic origin (unlike most other rocks) and those in the region were laid down in an orderly sequence with little disturbance.

Synonymous with discoveries throughout the region are the names of two archaeologists, Louis and Mary Leakey. In 1976, Mary Leakey discovered, south of Olduvai, a trail of footprints in the bed of volcanic ash which had been preserved for millions of years.

The footprints were left by *Australopithecus afarensis*, the precursor of several other hominids forms, including

Australopithecus boisei, Homo habilis, Homo erectus, Homo sapien and today's *Homo sapien sapien.*

Australopithecus, which means southern ape, lived one-and-a-half to four million years ago although the first primates to which hominids are linked had been living in the African forests for some 65 million years.

These early, mainly nocturnal primates had gradually developed hands to grip the branches, to scratch, to prey upon insects, and to test the ripeness of fruit. A hand-to-brain nerve system would have developed and this may have contributed to the expansion of the brain and its functions. Many of the characteristics we

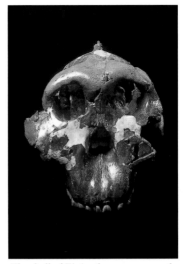

The skull of Zinjanthropus, commonly known as the Nutcracker Man

now accept and share with other primates began to develop, such as sensitive finger tips, three-dimensional binocular vision, an enlarged brain, and thumbs which enhance a powerful and precise, manipulative grip.

Our ancestors are believed to have descended from the trees adapting themselves increasingly to more open country. One theory holds that the reason they adapted to walking upright is that they were too short to see over the surrounding grasses and shrubs.

About two million years ago the brain of one hominid line began to evolve and its body to develop. This is the point when scientists accord our ancestors the more dignified name of *Homo* which long pre-dated gender awareness and literally means "man".

It is an ironic footnote when there is still much talk of recent colonialism, that present scientific evidence indicates the first "colonisers" emerged from Africa one million years ago and that it was not until 50000 years ago that modern humans reached the Americas and Australasia.

The first outsider to realise the potential of Olduvai Gorge was a German, Professor Wilhelm Kattwinkel who, in 1911, literally stumbled on it by chance while collecting butterflies. Following his report, an expedition, supported by the Kaiser, was led by Professor Hans Reck in 1913 to collect more fossils.

The First World War brought German research to an end. But the Berlin Museum remained convinced that Olduvai might contain secrets which would help unravel the mysteries which then surrounded human origin.

The Leakeys

In 1931, Louis Leakey, a Kenyan pre-historian, led his first (poorly funded) expedition to Olduvai. The party immediately found an Acheulean hand-axe (an early two-faced tool with a rounded cutting edge). The find encouraged further excavation. But the finds in the next 28 years were largely limited to basic tools and the fossil remains of animals, many extinct while others were previously unknown. It was in this period that the remains of Dinotherium were found.

Then on 17 July 1959, Mary Leakey spotted an exposed skull at the site where the first Acheulean hand-axe had been found in 1931. The skull was named Zinjanthropus and was popularly known as the Nutcracker Man because of his large back teeth. Among scientists it was known as Zinj, that having been the name the earliest Arab traders gave to the East African coastline.

Zinjanthropus was a member of the pre-hominid line and the find did more to create controversy in the scientific community than it did to resolve the question as to the origins of humans.

The debate was finally laid to rest in 1960 with the discovery of *Homo habilis*. He was the earliest toolmaker, who was nicknamed the Handyman. This find tripled the previous known age of humans to around 1.75 million years.

Ngorongoro contains several other archaeological mysteries although they are much younger. Among these are the somewhat inaccessible habitation sites at Engaruka at the foot of the Gregory Rift Wall, 50 km to the north of Mto-wa-Mbu.

A series of huts, which were built with stone, were cut into the rocks of the Rift overlooking several hundred acres of irrigated fields.

The occupants left the site at least 500 years ago and their identity and reasons for leaving remain a mystery.

At Kondoa, 240 km south of Ngorongoro, there is the largest and most developed rock art gallery to be found in East Africa.

At the western end of the Oldoinyoogol Hills is the 80 m high Nasera Rock (so named by the Maasai because the streaks indicated marks or writing).

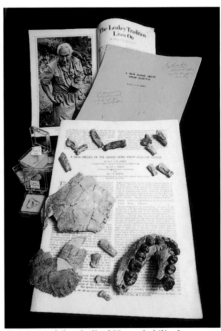

Portions of the skull of Homo habilis, known as Handyman, with a picture of Louis Leakey

Given this unique legacy of geological and archaeological sites, and the fact that Olduvai Gorge and Laitole are internationally noted sites, one must wonder why so few specialised or general archaeological tours visit the area, when the television audience in the United States alone was 27 million in November 1966 to watch the documentary *"Dr Leakey and the Dawn of Man"*.

Most visitors to Ngorongoro see only a fraction of the total Ngorongoro Conservation Area. They are usually restricted by time to the main road between the Lodoare entry gate, their hotel, the crater itself, and then the road onwards to the Serengeti Plains. But behind this lies a rich history.

The Ngorongoro geology, evolution, environment, mammals, birds, trees and shrubs are described in sections elsewhere. Here the history and compromises are detailed.

Human habitation in the area, as shown in the section on Evolution is relatively recent. Olduvai and the Laitole footprints, occurred millions of years earlier.

About 2000 to 3000 years ago, long before the Maasai arrived, the area was inhabited by an earlier group of pastoralists who, because of the stone bowls such as mortars they left behind, have become known as the Stone Bowl people.

Apart from cattle bones, revealing they were a pastoral people, they have left their mark through beads, pendants, pottery, stone tools and pieces of iron. On the side of *kopjes* sheltered from the prevailing wind, circles of stones, possibly used as cattle enclosures, can still be seen and they may have dug the original wells in shallow streams which the

Ngorongoro

Like many words (such as Kilimanjaro), the origin and meaning of the word Ngorongoro is shrouded in mystery.

Ngorongoro's first conservator, Henry Fosbrooke, wrote that the word is of Kalenjin (a Kenyan ethnic group) origin; and that the word, Gorongoro, Kerongoro or Korongoro, was dropped from Kalenjin vocabulary in disgrace some 200 years ago after the defeat by the Maasai of a warrior group using that name.

Such a claim is hotly disputed by some Maasai who do not acknowledge there were previous occupants at Ngorongoro. However, the Tatog-speaking Barabaig (an offshoot of the Kalenjin ethnic group), whom they are said to have defeated, regularly return to Ngorongoro for religious ceremonies at sacred shrines, and the Maasai acknowledge the Barabaig's warrior prowess.

Opposite page: The threatening glare of a leopard

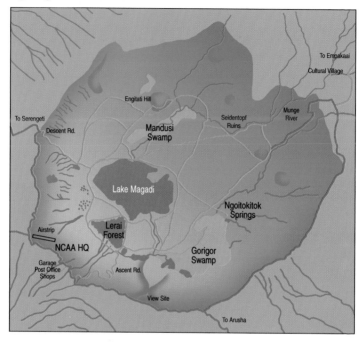

wildlife use today. Their dead were buried in communal graves covered with cairns of stones.

Then about 1000 years ago, as mysteriously as they had arrived, the Stone Bowl people vanished.

They would have overlapped with the Mbulu who are Cushitic people, thought to have originated in Ethiopia, and who began arriving in the area about 2000 years ago. The Mbulu, or more correctly Iraqw people, cultivated millet and kept cattle.

Today they are primarily cultivators living as far afield as Mbulu-Dongobesh with the farming town of Karatu as their capital.

Mbulu expansion was rebuffed some 300 years ago by the arrival in the area of the first Nilo-Hamitic group, the Barabaig, who kept cattle, were fearsome warriors, and who drove the previous occupants out of the Ngorongoro area. About 150 years ago, the Maasai, who still refer to the Barabaig as *mangati* meaning "a strong enemy", in turn supplanted them.

Engaruka

While much of this sequence has been unearthed by archaeologists, the origins and builders of the ancient ruins at Engaruka remain shrouded in mystery. Engaruka lies just east of the Gregory Rift some 50 km over a poor road which runs north from Mto-wa-Mbu.

The site is some five km in length and consists of a series of stone circles crafted on the gentle slopes at the base of the Rift. Many hundreds of platforms have been cut and hut sites built in the steeper slopes, and there are numerous burial sites marked by stone cairns.

On the plains below is a complex irrigation system covering two areas, each about 500 acres. These areas appear to have been irrigated by the Engaruka River which originates in the Ngorongoro Highlands and disappears into the sands of the Engaruka Depression.

Who exactly built Engaruka and why is not known. While the search for an explanation has focused on the existing people of the region, this neither explains the unique pottery found at Engaruka nor the fact that local people did not build with stone, as did people further south.

Another intriguing group of people who live in the Eyasi trough south-west of Ngorongoro Crater, are the Hadza or Watindiga. They are hunter-gatherers who speak a click language which was originally thought to be related to the click languages spoken by the southern African Khoisan (who are often referred to as Bushmen). Today the Hadza number only about 500 and their forebears may well be the earliest inhabitants of the area.

The Hadza are exceptionally gifted trackers and hunters whose skills are greatly valued by today's professional hunters. They smoke a tubular stone pipe, frequently containing marijuana, carry exceptionally tall six-and-a-half-feet long bows, and they are physically larger, stronger and darker-skinned than the southern African Khoisan.

Despite the Maasai's warrior prowess, smallpox, which killed the people, rinderpest which killed the cattle, locusts who consumed the grasslands, and drought, found the occupants of Ngorongoro ill-prepared to confront the latest invading group, the Europeans.

> ## Colonisation
>
> *Missionaries, traders, hunters, explorers and more openly-declared colonisers, invaded the area. They saw the Maasai as "noble savages" to be feared. But they took their most fertile lands. In Kenya 1904 and 1911 the Maasai were excluded from much of their dry season pastures and drought reserves, their former area becoming known as the "White Highlands". Instead the Maasai were relegated to the arid, government-controlled "Southern Reserve".*
>
> *Across the southern border in German East Africa (now mainland Tanzania), the Germans attempted to confine the Maasai to a reserve on the arid Maasai steppe south of today's Arusha-to-Moshi road. But the small German community was unable to enforce its policy. Instead piecemeal colonisation occurred. Maasai dry-season sanctuaries were taken by the white settlers on the slopes of Mount Kilimanjaro and elsewhere.*

The Maasai were also not allowed to use much of the crater by the Siedentopf brothers, Adolph and Friedrich Wilhelm, who began farming.

Germany's defeat in the First World War brought in the British as rulers of the mandated trust territory. One of the first written references to Ngorongoro is of the shooting of a sleeping rhino on the outskirts of a camp. This, "showed conclusively that [the] shooting and photography of wild animals" were incompatible, a member of the hunting party wrote.

The Maasai, confronted with what is kindly described as British "benign neglect", initially fared marginally better. A Maasai District, covering most of Tanganyika's Maasailand, was created in 1926. Agricultural encroachment onto pastoral lands was controlled and the Maasai prospered well into the 1930s.

An elephant browses on the crater rim oblivious to the watching people

Then, with war clouds gathering over Europe again, another phase of land alienation occurred. Higher productivity and bigger returns were the slogans of the time as a new wave of colonialism swept the region. Maasai grazing lands were expropriated to create ranches and a vast wheat scheme was begun to help feed the Allied forces fighting Germany and Italy in faraway Europe.

The Maasai Development Plan was launched in 1950. It was supposed to modernise the traditional pastoral economy by combating tsetse fly and providing water. Within five years the programme collapsed, its only lasting effect being even greater resource depletion.

The Serengeti-Ngorongoro area had been recognised as a prime wildlife area by early hunter-gatherers, pastoralists and then the European colonisers. Germany drew up the first fragmented legislation to protect the area's wildlife. But this was never implemented. The Game Conservation Ordinance was introduced by the British in 1921. In 1928 Ngorongoro was made a closed reserve where hunting and agriculture were forbidden. In 1930 this was extended to the Serengeti, although "sport" hunting continued in the reserves.

However, hunting in the reserves became increasingly uncontrolled and the area was declared a reserve under a new game protection ordinance in 1940. The park boundaries were revised in 1948, although it was to be three years before these boundaries were legally enforced.

That legislation did not affect the rights and livelihood of those living inside the park; on the contrary they were explicitly protected. Maasai elders were assured that their rights to live and subsist in the park would not be interfered with. But the die had already been cast and increasing restrictions on hunting, settlement, stock movement and fire-setting soon followed.

Confronted by mounting protest, the British published a White Paper in 1956. This proposed dividing the then existing Serengeti National Park into three smaller parks: the Serengeti much as it is today; the Ngorongoro Crater and Northern Highland Forest Reserve; and, finally, Empakaai Crater in the northeast near Engaruka.

Voice in the dark

While deprived pastoralists had made the initial protest leading to the White Paper, European and North American conservationists now added their voices, and to appease them an international committee of inquiry was set up. As a result, the existing Serengeti National Park was split in two, the western part kept the park's name, while the eastern plains, the Kakesio-Endulen area, and the whole of the highlands, formed the Ngorongoro Conservation Area.

The Maasai living in the Serengeti National Park were persuaded to move to the new Ngorongoro Conservation Area. They were promised permanent land rights and water supplies. The area represented an experiment in multiple land-use where the Maasai, tourist, pastoralist, cultivator, wildlife, and archaeological interests were all to be protected.

Inevitably conflicts arose between pastoralists and conservationists with the resulting shrinkage of grazing land, and in the late 1970s the grazing and watering (except during droughts) of livestock on the crater floor was prohibited. Cultivation within the conservation area was prohibited in 1975.

The Ngorongoro Conservation Area Authority (NCAA) now plays a leading role in the changes bringing practice in line with policy. Conservation requires the support of the indigenous and neighbouring people. Through a programme of education as to the value of their wildlife assets and of the resulting tourism, local attitudes are gradually changing.

Today the Maasai are allowed to take their livestock for water and to the salt licks around Seneto, but they may not reside or cultivate in the crater

THE MAASAI

When two Maasai meet the first greeting they exchange is *"Keserian ingera? Keserian ingishu? —* How are your wife and children? How are your cattle?" To have one without the other is to be poor. To have an abundance of both is to be rich.

When they pray they will say: "May God give you children, may God give you cattle". For the semi-nomadic pastoralist Maasai, whose lifestyle dictates that they must live in harmony with their environment, the value of children and cattle are symbiotic.

The cattle lack productivity when compared to most domestic stock. But they are sturdy and disease resistant. They culturally represent wealth and status in the Maasai society and are used as a medium of exchange, as well as to legitimise marriages. Cattle do not just give meaning to life, they are life.

Maasai means a speaker of the Maa language which has several dialects and is a spoken not a written language. This accounts for the variations in spelling. Linguistically, they are closest to the Bari of Sudan. The Maasai's nomadic ways, and aversion to being counted, have made an accurate census difficult, but it is thought that they number 300000 to 400000 in northern Tanzania and southern Kenya, of whom over 40000 live at Ngorongoro.

Maasai origins

The Maasai are thought to be a hybrid of Nilotes (from the River Nile regions) and Hamites (originating from North Africa). Their togas and sandals, the warriors' helmet-shaped hair styles, and the short, stabbing swords worn in red sheaths on their belts, all bear remarkable similarities to those of the ancient Romans who once occupied North Africa.

The origins of the Maasai are thought to have been in North Africa from where, along the River Nile, they migrated into East Africa about the 15th century, initially settling in the Lake Turkana area in Kenya. They are thought to have arrived in the Serengeti and Ngorongoro area in the 17th century, finally defeating the incumbent, pastoral Tatog groups, ancestors of today's Barabaig, in the 1830s.

Opposite page: A Maasai moran (warrior) with his distinctive hair style

Their homeland is broken into roughly 12 regions, the largest being Kisongo in Tanzania. Each region has its own people, name, leadership, dialect, ceremonies and ways of building houses.

The Tanzanian Maasai, less exposed to western influences than their Kenyan counterparts, retain closer ties with their fading traditions. The Ilkisongo prefer dark red and dark blue beadwork whereas the Kenyan Ilpurko like orange and light blue.

Dress also differs from region to region. The Ilkisongo favour below-the-knee togas while most Kenyan warriors prefer shorter more revealing togas which expose their bodies and are more photogenic for tourists.

Maasai in all areas daub their bodies with ochre, a finely ground red mineral mixed with animal fat or water. However, the Ilkisongo prefer a reddish-brown ochre while other regions favour a dark, blood-red hue.

The greatest difference, however, lies in the distinction in the way of life between the five Maasai groups. The "authentic" Maasai and the Samburu continue their semi-nomadic, pastoralist lives while the Baraguyu (Ilumbwa), Wa-Arusha and Njemps are more educated, settled and practise agriculture. The former disapprove of the latter saying they have abandoned their traditions while the latter argue that the former are primitive.

Standing stork-like, often on one leg supported by their long spears, the Maasai with their slim bodies, narrow waists and Nilotic features are readily recognisable and appear somewhat intimidating and unsmiling.

They believe that all cattle in the world belong to them and will rustle livestock from their neighbours. They are among the largest cattle owning people in Africa.

Their herds include sheep and goats, which are kept for their economic value and used ceremonially, as well as donkeys to haul water and firewood. Their cattle carry the brands of the five Maasai clans while smaller brands show individual ownership.

From their cattle the Maasai get their staple diet, milk, which they drink fresh, or sour like yoghurt.

Babies are fed ghee which is a clarified butter. Rarely, except during birth, illness, retreats, or ceremonies, are cattle killed.

Then the meat is shared, but milk and meat must

A Maasai woman and her ornate beadwork

not be eaten together as this is believed to cause tapeworms in humans and swollen udders in cows. More important is the belief that the milk of the living beast should not be drunk at the same time as the meat of a same beast is eaten.

During the dry season, when the cattle produce little or no milk, the Maasai drink the cattle's blood. The tip of an arrow is inserted in the jugular vein of the living animal and blood is drawn off. This is believed to give strength to warriors, assist women in birth and heal the wounded. Blood is also used during circumcision ceremonies.

However, their food does not derive exclusively from livestock. While milk, meat and blood are ideal, the Maasai will supplement their diet with grain.

The urine of the cattle also has several uses. The Maasai believe urine has medicinal properties, they wash calabashes in urine, and use urine to seal houses. Cattle horns and hooves are used as containers and trinkets, and the hides for clothing, shoes, bed covers and ropes.

For the Maasai their domestic livestock are of special significance. Their kraals or *engang* are designed in such a way that the cattle are protected at the centre of the thorn bush ring of huts while humans sleep on the outer perimeter. Every animal is personally known and loved for, as a Maasai saying goes, "God gave us cattle and grass — without grass there are no cattle, and without cattle there are no Maasai".

The reference to grass is important. The Maasai's domestic stock, like the Serengeti migrating herds, are dependent upon the rains and the fresh, green grass that the rains nurture. The environment in which they live determine the Maasai's way of life and seasonal movements.

The rainy season *(alari)* from November is an occasion for singing and feasting, and initiation ceremonies are at their peak. The dry season *(alamei)* can bring despair and death.

The two faces of God

God (Engai) is another fundamental element which dominates Maasai life. The Maasai believe in a single God, who may be a man or a woman, who lives both on earth and in heaven, and who has two distinct faces. They consciously separate these faces and actions into separate entities which resemble God and Satan.

The first is a black, good and benevolent God (Narok) who brings the thunder and rain which in turn brings grass for the cattle and prosperity for the people. The other God (Na-nyokie), is red and fearsome, the purveyor of lightning which maims and kills, and of the extreme dry season which brings famine and death. God is omnipresent, the determiner of life and death.

Opposite page: Maasai warriors against the backdrop of Serengeti

For the Maasai, life is in three stages or age-sets, rather like the Class of 97 concept or graduate of a specific school or college the western visitor will be more familiar with. These stages are childhood, warriorhood and elderhood.

In the first, boys will be seen herding livestock while girls assist their mothers. Warriors are sub-divided into junior and senior warriors, together forming one generation or age-set. Roughly every 15 years a new generation of warriors comes of age and each age-set is given its own name. Warriors graduate to elders who are again sub-divided into juniors and seniors with ancient elders retiring from the active direction of Maasai affairs.

These stages are marked by four initiation ceremonies for male Maasai. The first is *Alamal Lengipaata* just before circumcision for boys. Next comes *Emorata* which is the actual circumcision ceremony as the Maasai moves from childhood to warriorhood. *Eunoto* signifies the graduation to junior elderhood and *Olngesherr* the confirmation of senior elderhood.

A Maasai elder in his cultural village waits for tourists

At Ngorongoro, Maasai from all five clans are encountered although only the "authentic" Maasai are readily recognisable. It is necessary to first understand their history to understand their circumstance today.

In the 1890s, the Maasai were struck by several disasters. First came drought and famine, succeeded by smallpox. Rinderpest, which killed the cattle herds, followed, and finally vast swarms of locusts devoured the remaining grasslands.

These disasters coincided with the European "Scramble for Africa", and the European invaders, whose earlier contacts had introduced smallpox, found the Maasai weakened and only able to offer token resistance.

Colonialism in Kenya and Tanganyika, and a series of blatantly one-sided treaties, curtailed the movement of the Maasai. This resulted in their losing their best, dry season-retreat lands to new European settlers whom the British Governor described as being "superior races".

Such alienation was to continue through colonial times culminating in the 1958 agreement signed by 12 Maasai elders renouncing all rights to occupancy and grazing within the re-drawn Serengeti National Park.

Given the progressive alienation of their lands over the previous 70 years in the interests of modernisation, it is not difficult to imagine the wearied resignation of the elders when confronted with yet another *fait accompli*. This effectively decreed that where wildlife areas are concerned, human, and particularly African, rights were of secondary consideration.

As a result of the agreement, over 1000 Maasai, with 25000 cattle and 15000 goats and sheep, vacated the western Serengeti and were resettled in the Ngorongoro Conservation Area where they were promised permanent rights to the land and water supplies in return for the area they had lost.

In the 1970s, however, the Maasai range was reduced even further with an order prohibiting them from grazing and settlement on the crater floor although continued watering and salt licking was permitted. Cultivation within the conservation area was also forbidden.

THE CRATERS

Ngorongoro Crater evokes the image of Aladdin and his magic lamp. Polish the lamp and an amazing world of riches unfolds before your eyes. The difference, however, is that you do not need a magic lamp and the world of make-believe at Ngorongoro. What you see is real.

The landscape, as well as the density and diversity of wildlife in the 261 sq km crater, is unrivalled. From the rim the view below is hypnotic. And, as one descends, the microscopic, dark dots on the plains define themselves as living creatures. Viewed through a lens-finder or the naked eye, this is a Garden of Eden, beautiful and irresistible.

The only descent on the southern side of the crater is located on the road to Serengeti eight km from the main Ngorongoro lodges and camps. The vehicle travels along the crater's southwestern rim with the Malanja Depression, a deep bowl rising to a series of undulating hills dominated by Mount Makarut, on your left. Beyond are the plains where Maasai graze their livestock, Olduvai Gorge, and the Serengeti National Park.

Zebra are seen in this area amidst Maasai livestock, and elephant wander through the area with their stately, rolling gait seeming oblivious to everyone unless threatened. Reedbuck, water buck, leopard and hyena, after dawn and towards dusk, may also be seen.

Montane forest

The mixed high montane forest found in the area of the conservation headquarters, lodges and camps gives way on the southern crater rim to highland grassland dominated by dense tussocks of Eleusine jaegeri known in Maasai as Makutian grass, and Pennisetum schimperi or wire grass.

Scattered single trees or clumps of forest are found in this area with the dominant tree being Nuxia congesta. This is a large tree with a fluted and often gnarled trunk, and its presence here would suggest that this less fire susceptible tree is the survivor of a high montane forest and that other less resistant trees succumbed to fire.

Opposite page: A black-maned lion looks for his next meal

The crater is accessed through Windy Gap. The precipitous road which winds its way down the crater face was once an animal track and most of it is only wide enough for one vehicle.

If you can focus your eyes on more than the narrow road, and your mind on more than your concern about the vehicle's brakes and steering, the flora and fauna during your descent is captivating.

To your left, 600 m below, is the crater. On both sides of the road, shrub-land dominated by aromatic *Lippia javanica* with yellow-throated white or cream flowers and short spikes.

Aloe Secundiflora

Towering over the shrubs, and most noticeable to the right halfway down the descent, are dark-green *Euphorbia bussei* and *Euphorbia candelabrum* which grow up to 18 m in height. Often the branches are at the top; they have yellow green flowers and red fruit. The white sap is dangerous to open wounds or eyes. A mix of the pith of branches is used by Maasai women after childbirth.

During and after the rains many flowers can be seen during the descent. These include the pink lily, the single red flowers of *Kleinia Gregorii*, yellow flowering *Conyza hypoleuca,* and on the crater floor during the rains, there is a profusion of the pink-white flowering *Cyenium tubolosom.*

Just before you get to the bottom of the descent, there are colonies of large, untidy grass nests of Rufous-tailed weavers in the acacia trees on your left. This weaver, which has tawny-rufous colouring in the tail and wings, and brown body feathers, is found only in northern Tanzania. It can be very tame, and feeds on the ground, either alone or with starlings and Buffalo weavers.

Weavers, typified by their thick bills and strong legs, are often hard to tell apart. They are usually noisy and gregarious, and in Africa over 100 species have been identified, about half of these in Tanzania.

It will probably be with some relief that first-time visitors reach the crater floor. Tour vehicles usually pause and an ivy-covered toilet is discreetly located in the shade of a tree. Maasai herd their livestock to the nearby Seneto springs and salt licks at the foot of the crater, making the climb back to the rim at midday.

With reason the crater floor boasts the world's most intense and diverse collection of wildlife, some 25000 mammals during peak periods when the migratory species and residents intermingle on the crater floor.

Which route one chooses to explore the crater's 76 km of dirt (murram) roads, and in the dry season the 120 km of dry season tracks, is optional.

Protecting the environment

Off-the-road driving is strictly prohibited, as is camping on the crater floor. There are heavy fines for off-the-road driving and visitors should discourage their drivers from breaking this law. These measures are intended to reduce disturbance to the seemingly almost tame wildlife, control soil erosion, and improve the visitor's experience.

However, the number of vehicles at one time on the crater floor (140 have been recorded!) is excessive and a rationing system and maximisation of vehicle carrying loads is to be introduced. This vehicle density is irritating when a rarer or more sought after species such as lion, cheetah, leopard, elephant or rhinoceros is sighted.

Such sightings draw tourist vehicles and there are frequently long lines, with tourists hanging out of windows or peering from the raised roofs through cameras or binoculars. The animals seem unperturbed by this intrusion on their privacy and lion, rhinoceros and elephant wander among the vehicles.

If the visitors' vehicle starts off in a clockwise direction from the foot of the Seneto descent, herds of plains' game such as wildebeest, zebra and Thomson gazelle will be encountered almost immediately.

Buffalo population

Ten years ago, although there was ample grass, buffalo shunned the crater floor, preferring the habitat of the forested rim. Why the buffalo have changed their habitat has not yet been established. Today they number some 4500 on the crater floor. The larger herds you will see will almost certainly be females with calves. Male buffalo, particularly those beyond breeding age, spend their retirement in smaller groups, often in the crater's foothills. All look baleful and it is easy to understand why this is the most respected and feared animal in the bush.

Different vegetation communities are distinguishable in the crater. The eastern wall is dominated by high montane forest, diminishing to the south and west where the rainfall is much lower. This high montane forest is similar to that which the visitor drives through from the Lodoare Gate and it is the water source for Ngoitokitoki Springs in the south of the park where many visitors picnic at lunchtime.

Fire-resistant bush occupies the area around the outer edges of the crater. Beneath this ring, flowers such as the daisy-like *Aspilia mossambicensis* and *Euphorbia* dominate, emphasising the dryness of these areas. Also common in the Seneto area are two types of trees, the fleshy-leaved *Synadenium grantii* and pawpaw-like clusters of leaves of the *Cussonia holstii*. The more alert eye may spot mountain reedbuck camouflaged among the vegetation.

Grasslands cover the largest area of the crater, and grass plays a vital part in determining the species which reside here. Most of the grasses are perennial, able to spread and maintain themselves without the use of seed.

Buffalo are found on the crater floor and forested surrounds

In contrast, annual grasses are found in eroded areas where the more stable perennials have not established themselves.

The relationship between grasslands and mammals is an important part of nature's complex cycle. When the grass is green during the rains the grazing herds are spread throughout the crater. In the dry season, the grass in the centre crater floor dries up becoming unpalatable, and the herds retreat to the swamp surrounds or crater slopes in pursuit of greener pastures.

There are also the differing preferences of some herbivores, both in the grass they eat and the denser cover they avoid where they are vulnerable to predators. Zebra first utilise denser, high grass. Once they have reduced its height, wildebeest and gazelle enter the scene. Each crops the grass further down before moving on.

This interaction on the grassland mosaic leads to varying degrees of greenness, palatability, height, density, age, and use by the herbivores. Grazing pressures, fire and drought also determine the amount of pasture for the herbivores.

Less palatable grasses, such as wire grass and *Pennisetum mezianum* or bamboo grass are most frequently found on the crater slopes. On the floor of the crater *Themeda triandra* or red oats grass is more common and palatable to the herbivores. Several species of dropseed or *Sporobolus sp.* are found in the more alkaline areas around the lake edge and in the drier southwestern part of the crater.

Around the hippopotamus pools another type of grass occurs. This is a pioneer grass *Odyssea Paucinervis,* which colonises the bare soil sending out shoots which in turn send out additional shoots. Other grasses move in, colonising the initial coloniser, which then moves on to new bare patches of ground as the water recedes.

The heavily tusked elephant and (inset) his closest relative, the tiny rock hyrax

Another vegetation form is the woodland, distinct from the high montane forest, with fewer trees and less complicated structure and density. Two types of this woodland occur in Ngorongoro Crater and in each case there is a distinctive tree species.

The north wall of the crater is occupied by *Acacia lahai* or red thorn acacia which is gradually taking over the niche of the high montane forest in the east and which abruptly gives way to grass and bush in the more fire-vulnerable west of the crater. Elephant damage, hanging, torn bark, may be seen. Steinbok are resident, and the heads of giraffe, who do not venture into the crater, possibly because of its steep sides and limited suitable vegetation, may be seen above the rim.

The Lerai Forest, between Lake Magadi and the ascent road, is a ground-water forest dependent upon the high water-table and the springs above in the crater wall, and not on the nearby lake and swamp. Surrounding the area is red oats grassland, and the forest is dominated by yellow-barked fever trees, *Acacia xanthophloea* which take their Maasai names from the presence of malaria in this mosquito-breeding, swampy area.

The swamps, and several small lakes during the rainy season, are essential components to the maintenance of the density of wildlife. The Mandusi Swamp in the north is fed by the Munge River while the Gorigor Swamp in the southeast is fed by the Lonyonyokie River.

During the dry season, when grass in much of the crater is dry and unpalatable, the grass around these swamps is green and moist, and some 80 per cent of the wildlife population is to be found in these two areas.

A moving forest

As is so often the case with nature, something inexplicable is happening in the Lerai Forest. The forest is very gradually moving from its present location to a nearby well-drained area.

Although the yellow-barked fever trees are groundwater dependent, Acacia xanthophloea seems not to be. This is why there are an abundance of old dead trees in the forest and few seedlings.

Bohor reedbuck and rhinoceros are found around the Mandusi Swamp and elephants cross the crater floor from Lerai Forest to the north wall where they feed on *Aeschynomene schimperi* thicket.

A deep pool exists between Gorigor Swamp and Lerai Forest and here hippopotamus and the occasional fish eagle may be seen.

Reeds dominate this water area including *Cyperus papyrus* which in ancient times was used to make parchment and later the first paper.

Olmoti and Empakaai Craters

In the northeast of the crater there is a single ascent and descent road which leads through the large Maasai village of Nainokanoka and onto Olmoti, the Embulbul Depression and Empakaai. These sites can also be approached by the road running around the eastern side of the crater rim but this road is less good and interesting than the drive across Ngorongoro Crater floor (see map on page 36).

After you leave the crater floor past Silalei Hill, which is identifiable by the quarry near its top, the climb to the crater rim takes about 45 minutes. The road passes through forests of twisted *Acacia lahai*. The road forks left at the first junction to Nainokanoka village and right to the Sopa Lodge and the route back to the main road through forest and moors.

After this you can proceed onwards to Nainokanoka village and take the last track out of the village on your left leading to the rangers' camp. Here the vehicle can be parked and a guide hired for the 30-minute walk to the rim of Olmoti. It is as well to hire a guide to ensure you take the right track and do not run into buffalo.

Cultural village

Take the road left to Irkeepus and Nainokanoka villages. As you approach the first village [Irkeepus], look to your right and you will see a Maasai cultural boma where you can take photographs, purchase Maasai handicrafts and watch the traditional dances.

Olmoti Mountain is neither high nor steep. The crater floor is shallow, covered by clumps of grass; Maasai livestock, buffalo, eland and reedbuck may be seen. The water flowing across the crater floor meets on the south side plunging over a spectacular waterfall several hundred metres into the ravine below.

This is the birthplace of the Munge River which tumbles on down into the Ngorongoro Crater where it feeds the Mandusi Swamp and goes onwards into Lake Magadi providing its source of fresh water.

Munge is a Maasai word which refers to the Black and White Colobus monkey hair anklets they once wore. But this distinctive monkey, with its cape of long white hair, is today not found closer than Mount Meru just outside Arusha town, although the word *Munge* would suggest these monkeys once existed around Olmoti.

At Nainokanoka village the visitors rejoin their vehicles and proceed on a dirt road towards Empakaai. Like Ngorongoro, the views of this crater are sensational and it is a pity that it is so far off the beaten tourist track and that so few people see it.

A Coke's hartebeest

In the 1950s it was proposed that Empakaai Crater become a national park in its own right. But instead it was incorporated in the Ngorongoro Conservation Area and, given limited resources, has not as yet developed its potential as a major tourist destination.

The crater, most of the year, is a verdant paradise. Like Ngorongoro it is really a caldera, some six km wide, half of which is filled by an unusual 85 m deep lake comprising a mix of fresh and soda water. The forest-clad walls of the caldera rise nearly 300 m from the crater floor in places.

Empakaai is visible on a clear day from a considerable distance. At the crater rim the vehicle is once again parked and the western side climbed on foot. During the rains, there are a profusion of flowers such as the readily identifiable *Kniphofia* or red-hot poker, delphiniums, everlastings and gladioli. Brilliantly coloured sunbirds, seeking nectar through their long beaks, zero in on clumps of orange-flowered *Leonotis* or lions paw.

A track, which sometimes is blocked by falls or eroded, continues around the 32-km crater lip affording spectacular views. To the northeast is the still active volcano, Oldoinyo Lengai and beyond Lake Natron just inside Tanzania close to the Kenyan border.

The visitor to Empakaai is advised to camp in the area for a day or two. There is a basic cabin on the southern shores of the crater lake which can be used with permission from the conservation authority and water can be obtained from a spring nearby for cooking and washing. But the visitor is advised to bring drinking water. June, July and August are cold months and warm clothing and bedding are essential. Frequently the mornings are blanketed in swirling mist which clears in the afternoons leaving magnificent, clear views of the crater and night sky.

This is a remote, pristine place where the visitor truly gets away from everything. The dark red-brown and crooked boles of *Hagenia abyssinica* trees dominate the woodland. Buffalo, bushbuck and blue monkey are among the mammals likely to be seen, and flamingo exist in abundance at certain times of the year along the lake's serene and placid foreshore.

Masek and Ndutu (Lagarja) Lakes

As you drop down from Ngorongoro towards the Serengeti Plains, and just before the Serengeti National Park boundary, a track forks to your left six km past the Olduvai Gorge junction. This track runs just inside the Ngorongoro boundary. A second track into the same area branches off four km from Naabi Hill Gate inside the Serengeti.

Home pasture

In the area through which these two tracks pass to Lakes Masek and Ndutu (or Lagarja) you will encounter some of the 2.5 million wildebeest, zebra, Thomson's gazelle and Grant's gazelle on the short grass plains from late November through May just before the migration proper begins. This is their home pastureland, the only place of any protracted residence.

When the grass and water is exhausted, the wildebeest and zebra are the first to migrate to the woods and western plains in the Serengeti. The gazelle, along with eland, remain longer, obtaining moisture from the yellow or two-tone green *Solanum* or Sodom Apples which grow on the small bushes along the road and on the plains.

Migration route

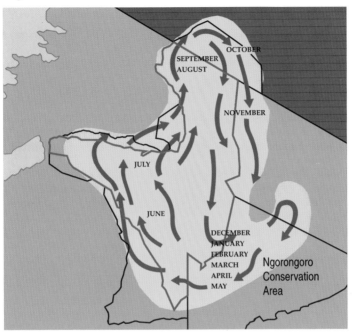

The plains around Masek and Ndutu are the area where the vast herds
re-group, regain their strength, mate and finally calve, before their 2000
km migration. The short rains, usually expected in November, transform
this area's arid, dusty plains bringing new green grass and water which
draws the hungry and thirsty herds.

Predicting exactly where the herds will be at a given time is impossible.
This is dictated by the rains (which are never the same in consecutive
years), with the resulting availability of grass and water.

The continual ebb and flow of the herds is easily confused with the
migration. Thus the preceeding map should be regarded as a guideline
and not definitive.

Wildebeest

The White Bearded Wildebeest, whose scientific name is *Connochaetes taurinus,* is affectionately known as "The Clown of the Plains" because of its comic behaviour. It was once said of this lovable but scatter-brained creature that it had been "designed by a committee and assembled from spare parts".

If so, they have proved remarkably durable. Fossil remains found in the Olduvai Gorge area, through which the wildebeest pass during their migration, show that they have remained virtually unchanged physically for some two million years. Today they continue to embrace and connect the area's ecosystem which includes Ngorongoro.

On the plains, solitary bulls snort noisily as their strength flows back and they stage mock battles for territory, while the females and calves graze, ignoring their antics. But virtually any excuse will suffice for the bulls to break off an encounter and then proceed as if it never occurred.

White Bearded Wildebeest

Wildebeest are gregarious characters with their social structure headed by a territorial male who guards a small area and tries to attract females to it. The territorial bulls mark their territories by rubbing their face glands in the grass, and younger bulls will try to drive the incumbent off.

Defending territory is a time-consuming as well as somewhat ritualistic exercise. The wildebeest's threat posture is neck held erect, head horizontal and a "rocking-horse" canter all of which sounds fairly unintimidating but which is remarkably successful in deterring most would-be invaders. If this fails the contending bulls drop to their knees with their "bosses" (the bony protuberance between the horns) noisily clashing. But even these encounters are seldom serious and injuries rare.

Another highly notable event during the rains in this area is the crossing and re-crossing of the lakes by tens of thousands of wildebeest.

There is no apparent reason for this suicidal venture other than the wildebeest's apparent unwillingness to make a detour around the lakes believing that a straight line is the fastest way between two points, in this case areas of grass.

When the wildebeest stampede, which is not uncommon and occurs for no particular reason, lines of swimming wildebeest pass each other in the lakes.

Snorting mothers seek their lost calves and pitifully bleating calves search for their mothers. Thousands may drown as the senseless ritual plays itself out.

Calves who have lost their mothers may follow cars or come right into camps. Some will eventually find their mothers, others will perish. No one adopts the lost orphans. That is nature's dictate. But even in death the carcasses

Mating and birth

During the mating phase, bulls advance on the females with lowered heads and swishing tails. Then the bull circles, their bodies low and tail streaming, and, amidst grunting and bawling, endeavour to chase the female onto their territory. Poaching females from other bulls territories is continuous and the avaricious bull is in perpetual motion circling his own herd and seeking new wives while fighting off other bulls.

This mating or rutting occurs in April/May and some females will mate with several bulls. Gestation takes 250 days with the female normally detaching herself from the herd and lying down to give birth to a calf weighing about 22 kg. Calves have only minutes to stand and learn to run to keep up with the herds and to try to avoid the ever-lurking predators which include lion, cheetah, leopard, hyena, jackal and even baboon.

Around 250000 calves are born each year. For some inexplicable reason, 65 per cent of them are female and only 35 per cent male. This helps maintain the bull wildebeest's polygamous preferences.

serve a purpose; the meat food for the vultures and the predators, the bleached bones camouflaged nesting sites for tiny sand plovers. The weak and the strong are separated and the plains become marginally less crowded.

Much of this activity occurs during the months when overseas visitors generally do not visit the area, probably because they are deterred by the rainy season and are unaware of the spectacle they are missing. Usually, despite the rains, the roads remain passable and for the few visitors this is a memorable period.

Zebra

Behind, or in the lead, zebra are inevitably intermingled with wildebeest although they forego some of the wildebeest's more idiosyncratic habits. Unmistakable by their pony-like physical appearance and black and white stripes, the zebra is a member of the *Equidae* family which crossed into North Africa from Europe some 15 million years ago.

A zebra mother and foal

From their earliest known ancestor, *Hipparion primigenium*, remains of which have been found in East Africa, they gradually evolved into the Burchell's Zebra which can be seen in the region today.

Stallions dominate the zebra family which is usually found on the savannah plains where the animals are mainly grazers.

They live in family groups which consist of the stallion, one or more mares, and foals. Rejected stallions form bachelor groups.

They are rarely found far from water and have acute hearing, sight and smell. Their *kwa-ha-ha* call is part of Africa's melody.

Fighting zebra

Despite their deference to almost all other species, zebra can be very vicious in defence of their foals and in fights between males, who rear, teeth bared, biting and kicking, blood can flow freely. Generally, however, they are placid, ever-alert and gallop away at the slightest hint of danger.

Gestation takes 360 to 390 days and foals are born throughout the year with the peak in December/January when they are in their non-migratory months. Foals weigh 30 to 35 kg and the herd stands protectively by while a mare gives birth.

Gazelle

There are two species of gazelle found in the area, Grant's *(Gazella granti)* and Thomson's *(Gazella thomsoni)* which are often found together, but are easily differentiated.

Grant's are much larger, lighter in colour, their horns are longer and splay outwards and they lack the conspicuous flank-band and dark stripe on the rump patch which is found on the Thomson's.

Thomson's, or "Tommies", are one of the most attractive and delicate animals seen in the area. They are East Africa's most populous gazelle with loose, constantly changing herds of up to 60, comprising females and young led by an older female and accompanied by a single mature male.

A Grant's gazelle (left) and a smaller Thomson's (right)

When alarmed, Thomson's flee in a series of bounds called "spronking" or "stotting" which involves the legs and head remaining stiff as they spring up and down rather like mobile rocking horses. Thomson's are comparatively silent with keen sight and smell.

Grant's which can weigh three times as much, have very similar habits to Thomson's although their herds are smaller, and they make a grunt or bleat when alarmed in contrast to the Thomson's which does not make a discernible noise and seems to signal danger through flicking its flanks.

Birds

Throughout the year this area is a birder's paradise. In the rainy season, escaping the European winter, vast flocks of migrants arrive, notable among them tens of thousands of European white storks and smaller, purple and white Abdim's storks.

Three main European migration routes converge on this area bringing along them hordes of non-resident species such as terns, which will be found on water margins, kestrels, who, like the storks, hunt insects on the plains, and harriers. Pale blue European Rollers mix with the resident, chubby and conspicuous Lilac-breasted Rollers, and cuckoos from both Europe and India are among the many birds assembled in the area.

RHINOCEROS

Fossil remains reveal there were four related species of rhinoceros, *Aceratherium, Brachypotherium, Chilotherium* and *Dicerorhinus,* during the early Miocene Epoch 19 to 23 million years ago. Their predecessors, whose roots are presently speculative, lived during the preceding epoch originating some 60 million years ago.

In Africa today there are four agreed sub-species of black rhinoceros *(Diceros bicornis).* These are the northwestern group in Cameroon and the Central African Republic (where they may be extinct); the eastern group in Kenya and northern Tanzania *(Diceros bicornis michaeli);* a desert group in Namibia *(Diceros bicornis bicornis);* and the larger, bush population *(Diceros bicornis minor),* which occurs throughout southern Africa and stretches into southern Tanzania.

Only in Tanzania do two of the four African groups of black rhinoceros occur naturally in the wild and on the reverse side of the Tanzanian 50 shilling coin there is a female rhinoceros with a "tick bird" on her back and a calf, marking the country's unique place in Africa.

Three other rhinoceros species — in India, Java and Sumatra — survive today.

The reverse side of the Tanzanian 50 shilling coin

In Africa, both black and white rhinoceros exist and they have been virtually unchanged physically for four million years. Their size and strength was enough to protect them until they confronted the super-predator — humans — who possessed weapons and territorial ambitions.

The word, "rhinoceros", is of Greek origin, *rhino* meaning nose and *keras* meaning horn. Together with horses and tapirs (a rhinoceros-related, hoofed, pig-like mammal still found in South America and Malaysia), they originated in Europe. Their fossil remains have been found all over the world except in South America, Australia and Antarctica.

An adult black rhinoceros stands around 1.6 metres at the shoulder and weighs about 1000 kg. Its skin is thick with sparse hair covering. It has

eyelashes, hairy ear-fringes and hairy tips to its tail except when predators such as lion and hyena have hit and missed when it was a calf. Folded skin above the knees is notable on the front limbs and the skin is covered with sweat glands through which droplets appear when the animal is stressed.

Rhinoceros horns, erroneously valued as an aphrodisiac, are a mass of tubular filaments of a substance similar to hair. The horns sprout from the skin and are not attached to the bone below. But the bone underneath the horn is corrugated to allow the skin to be firmly attached. The front horn is usually larger, pointing forward while the rear horn tends to point upward.

Rhinoceros have three toes on their feet, the legs in the front being larger than the rear enabling them to carry the huge head, neck and shoulders. The cushioned foot pads, rather like car shock absorbers, have a mosaic of irregular cracks. By this means, as well as the larger nails of the white rhinoceros, it is possible to tell the tracks of the two species apart and to identify individual rhinoceros from their spoor.

Frequently rhinoceros will be seen with Redbilled or Yellowbilled Oxpeckers, known as "tick birds", perched on them.

Not black and white

The terms "black rhinoceros" and "white rhinoceros" are misleading, for both are dark grey. Like elephants, their skin colour is worn much like a garment and dictated by the soil where they live, with wallowing in mud or dust dramatically changing their outward appearance.

But they can be identified by the square lip of the white rhinoceros (Ceratotherium simum) in contrast to the hooked, prehensile upper lip of the black rhinoceros. White rhinoceros are grazers like cows, whereas black rhinoceros are mainly selective browsers with the hooked lip enabling them to grasp twigs.

There are other notable differences. The white rhinoceros is slightly taller with adult males weighing twice as much as their black cousins. The black rhinoceros also has a longer neck, smaller rounded ears and carries its head higher. The nuchal hump, evident on the nape of the neck of the white rhinoceros, is absent.

Opposite page: A black rhinoceros with the crater wall behind

They have a symbiotic relationship, with the birds feeding on ticks and flies and, in the case of South African black rhinoceros, the blood from lesions. The birds have a further value, their loud chattering and calls acting as an early warning of impending danger.

A black rhinoceros and zebra contentedly graze oblivious of each other

The black rhinoceros prefers a habitat which provides ample shrubs and young trees, usually not more than four metres high, thickets to shelter from the heat of the day or inclement weather, and water nearby to drink and wallow. For these reasons the Ngorongoro rhinoceros are frequently found in or near the Lerai Forest.

Black rhinoceros tend to "prune" the shrubs and small trees they feed on, often giving the sides and top a rounded, manicured look. The signs of the destruction wrought by elephants on the vegetation is absent, and generally rhinoceros show an aversion to dry plants.

Rhinoceros sleep during the heat of the day, either standing motionless, or lying down in an upright position with their legs curled underneath their bodies. Sometimes black rhinoceros sleep on their sides, a position the white rhinoceros do not emulate because they cannot roll over.

The black rhinoceros vocalises in a number of ways, the most common being a repeated, loud snort when an individual is frightened or angry. When fighting, they grunt and growl, and on other occasions including during mating, they may scream or squeal loudly.

Conventional wisdom is that black rhinoceros are solitary animals with the only stable bond being between mother and calf, terminating around the time the next calf is born. Other associations are transitory.

In the strictest sense, black rhinoceros are not territorial. But females tend to remain in their home or natal range, with the dominant male's territory encompassing that range. So, whilst the oldest rhinoceros, John did not regard Mikidadi as a threat, he certainly regarded Ngorongoro's other male, Runyoro, as such and there have been serious fights between them for dominance.

John, according to human accounts, has emerged victorious from these fights with Runyoro driven outside the females' home range to the northern part of the crater. For the moment, Mikidadi, who is probably John's son, does not pose a threat. But the time will come when he does, and one of the two will have to make way, killed in a fight or through emigrating.

John and Runyoro's fighting was one of the considerations in not reintroducing the orphaned Richard (his mother, Amina, was poached in September 1995) to the crater. Instead Richard (and one other rhinoceros given by Frankfurt Zoological Society) were translocated in November 1997 to South Africa in return for two females bringing the number of black rhinoceros at Ngorongoro to 17.

> ### Seven up
>
> *In Ngorongoro in November 1998, I photographed seven rhinoceros, a male and six females, together (see cover picture of this guide). The male was Mikidadi, apparently young enough not to be sexually threatening, who had been left as custodian of the females while the crater's dominant male, John, pursued another female in oestrus.*
>
> *Nevertheless, I am assured, sighting and photographing such a large group today is rare if not unique and the picture sent experts scurrying for their contemporary record books. Larger groups had been seen — but not in the past 25 years.*

The second consideration involved in the swap was the inter-breeding which could occur in the crater with the dominant male mating with his own female offspring. The introduction of a new female bloodline should bring greater genetic diversity.

Rhinoceros breed at any time of the year. Pre-oestrus lasts about a week with tail-erecting by females rather as one finds with dogs. Complex encounters between females and dominant males occur in this phase with the cow squirting small amounts of urine on the ground.

The bull's approach to the female is circumspect. With a stiff-legged gait, hind legs dragging on the ground, the bull approaches. Some sparring with the front horns and nudging with the side of their heads, may occur, while the bull may thrust his horn between the cow's hind legs and the cow may sometimes attack her suitor.

The oestrus cycle lasts about 35 days with prolonged copulation occurring frequently amidst much screaming and squealing. Gestation takes 15 months with a single calf being born weighing around 40 kg.

The calves suckle within three hours of birth and this continues for about a year. The calves are very alert and playful but they are vulnerable to predators, notably lion and hyena. The mother frequently display unusual intolerance to disturbance and threat, calling her calf with a high-pitched mew while the calf emits bellowing squeaks when lost. The close mother-calf relationship is abruptly terminated at about the point of birth of a new calf.

While calves are vulnerable to lion and hyena, adult rhinoceros generally disregard other large predators in their area. The rhinoceros' sight is poor, but their hearing and smell are acute and although they may look like cumbersome, prehistoric relics, they can move at surprising speed and turn within their own length.

Rhinoceros have a reputation of being irascible and bad-tempered but this is dictated by circumstance and by the individual. Generally they will move off at the smell of humans although a rhinoceros which has been hunted may charge from 70 m away. But they seldom press home the attack and will usually veer away at a loud shout.

A rhinoceros ignores the visitors

Poaching

Over a century ago Africa's rhinoceros were shot to the brink of extinction by European hunters. Now because of the fallacious belief that the shavings of rhinoceros horns increase sexual prowess and contain medicinal properties, as well as the demand for them as dagger handles in Yemen, the rhinoceros are once again seriously threatened.

In 1665, South Africa's founding white settler, Jan van Riebeeck, recorded black rhinoceros on the slopes of Cape Town's Table Mountain. By 1853 they had been exterminated. White rhinoceros were then abundant in southern and South Africa. However, the early European settlers developed a taste for rhinoceros meat, particularly the prized nuchal hump. They also used the hide to make sjamboks to whip the indigenous people.

In 1848, two South African white hunters killed 89 white rhinoceros on a short hunting trip. Another hunter shot 50 during a safari to Lake Ngami. In the early 1880s one store in South Africa stocked as many as 100 rhinoceros horns which were then fashionable for carved knife handles.

"Long before the close of the century the white rhinoceros will have vanished from the face of the earth," observed one writer. With a very few exceptions, the white rhinoceros was exterminated in southern Africa by the end of the 19th century. Today, however, the South African white rhinoceros population has recovered to over 4000 with smaller populations elsewhere.

Referring to East Africa, the British explorer, John Burton wrote in 1856, "The black rhinoceros with a double horn is as common as the elephant". But such abundance was to be short-lived. Sir John Willoughby and three other army officers shot 66 rhinoceros in the Taveta region in Kenya in four months. Count Teleki and his party, who "discovered" Lake Rudolph (now Lake Turkana), shot 99 during their journey. Another party killed 80 in less than three months.

In neighbouring German East Africa (now Tanzania), a Dr Kolb is credited with killing 150 before one killed him. His companion, Herr von Bastineller accounted for 140 and the German commandant of Moshi fort, Herr von Eltz, dispatched 60.

OTHER MAMMALS

The mammal population in Ngorongoro Crater has perceptibly changed in the past three decades. Not only has domestic livestock, with the exception of the area around Seneto Springs, been barred from the crater, but some species of wildlife have diminished in numbers. At the same time others have increased in numbers and new species have moved in.

Rhinoceros are a case in point. Their number is down from the 1966 high of 108 to 17 today. The number of wildebeest, in common with those throughout the ecosystem generally, are also down. In sharp contrast, Cape buffalo, who once utilised only the rim and rarely ventured onto the crater floor, are now present in their thousands, especially during the rains.

A hyena, awoken from his rest, lazily looks at the intruder

How much variation there has been in the number of big cats — lion, leopard and cheetah — is a more problematic question. The lions are conspicuous although even they can be well camouflaged.

The number today is around 50. They include Ngorongoro's famous and photogenic black-maned lions. The population of the crater is divided into five resident prides.

Nocturnal and secretive leopards are impossible to count and are more likely to be seen on the rim or crater slopes preferring this habitat which offers cover and trees to safely store food away from the unwelcome attentions of lion and hyena.

New residents

Cheetah, who were not resident in the crater a decade ago, possibly because of the concentration of lion and hyena which threaten them and their cubs, show signs of residence. A female was seen in the Munge River area early in 1997. Later she produced two cubs in the same area suggesting that she has, temporarily at least, taken up residence.

Another species not present 20 years ago on the crater floor was warthog. Today, although not in the abundance they will be seen on the Serengeti Plains, warthog have also taken up residence.

Some species, notable among them giraffe, impala, topi and oryx, still shun the crater floor which only makes up four per cent of the Ngorongoro Conservation Area. This, in turn is only a small portion of the entire Serengeti ecosystem.

The species absent from the crater will, however, be seen elsewhere, having adapted to other habitats.

The factors which led to the removal of livestock, and to the poaching of the rhinoceros, are directly attributable to humans. But to what extent, if at all, humans have played a role in other wildlife comings and goings is still impossible to answer completely.

However, the indications are, that the human decision to exclude the Maasai in 1974 from residence, and their livestock from grazing, plus the total banning of burning, led to a variation in the grasses in the crater which has in turn affected the number and diversity of species.

In January 1974 the number of wildebeest was over 16000 making them the largest species in terms of numbers as well as biomass. The latest counts by the Ngorongoro Ecological Monitoring Programme shows one-third of that number.

In January 1974 only 550 buffalo were counted during the wet season. The most recent wet season count showed they numbered over 3700 and the figure is higher than that today. A buffalo's weight is considerably in excess of the weight of a wildebeest which means in terms of biomass, if not actual numbers, they are now the dominant herbivore.

Some other grazers such as Thomson's gazelle and mixed grazers/browsers such as Grant's gazelle have had their numbers reduced in the same time frame. Thomson's have dropped dramatically from over 3500 to less than 1000 in the same period while the number of Grant's has significantly reduced, although less dramatically, from almost 1400 to just over 1100.

The long grass, with a high ratio of stem-to-leaf, which domestic livestock previously ate, is more to the liking of buffalo than wildebeest and similar or smaller bodied species such as Thomson's who prefer shorter, lower fibre grass.

So, it would appear, a human decision which was based on inadequate knowledge of the environment's complex web, has adversely affected the wildebeest, Thomson's and Grant's populations. But it has had a positive impact on the numbers of Cape buffalo, although it is suggested these may also have been fleeing agricultural encroachment outside the crater.

In contrast to these animals, most other non-migratory species have held their own or increased. The number of resident elephants, which are all bulls, has doubled through migration in the same two decades to almost 50 while the number of ostrich has tripled to almost 100. Hippopotamus are also increasing.

Ngorongoro Crater probably has the highest density of predators in the world. The number of spotted hyena may exceed 400. There are no statistics of the number of jackal with the golden (which is rare elsewhere) likely to be the species most frequently seen in the crater.

A mud-caked golden jackal

BIRDS

Over 550 bird species, some resident and others migratory, have been recorded in the Ngorongoro Conservation Area making this one of the world's prime destinations for birders as well as those who have come to view the caldera and its remarkable density and diversity of mammals.

Some birds are seed-eaters, more commonly found in open country. Generally they are smaller, less visually eye-catching LBJs (little brown jobs) tending to predominate. Others, often larger and more colourful, are fruit-eaters preferring the forest habitat. Another group, including vultures and eagles, prey on carrion and small reptiles. Yet another group are waterbirds feeding on fish, crustaceans and algae.

The most numerously recorded species at Ngorongoro numbering 17 are weaver, followed by cisticola and warbler at 16 each. Fifteen species of eagle have been identified as well as 14 of sunbird and plover, ten of heron, cuckoo, owl and swift, eight of kingfisher and nightjar and six of vulture.

The list goes on and on with a bewildering profusion of colours and calls evident. And, for the more specialised birder, there are the rarer species.

There are the birds endemic to northern Tanzania including Ngorongoro. They include the parrot-related and nutcracker-beaked Fischer's lovebird with its brilliantly coloured orange-red forehead, cheeks and throat and bright green plumage. The more dowdy Rufous-tailed weaver is also endemic to the region.

The "mega" bird

The translucently coloured Angola pitta or, as it has been recently renamed, the African pitta, which advanced "twitchers" pay thousands of dollars to see, is one of the species to be found at Ngorongoro.

This is not intended as a definitive ornithological text. Rather this guide seeks to highlight the rarer, most conspicuous and colourful birds you are likely to see, pinpoint their probable locality and provide information about some of them.

Opposite page: The magnificently coloured and adorned head of a Crowned crane

Ostrich, the world's largest bird, cannot fly but can run at 70 km an hour. It is present throughout the year and their mating dance is an elaborate and notable event. The black-feathered male is easily distinguishable from the brown-feathered female, and the males' necks redden as the mating season approaches.

The two to two-and-a-half metre tall birds weighing 130 kg, are totally uninhibited as they dance on the plains, their feathered wings and tails raised and waving. The male may be polygamous with their "wives" laying two dozen or more eggs in a shallow scraped nest on the ground. The male sits on the eggs by night, the female by day. The eggs and chicks are both preyed upon and the ostrich, kicking with its long sturdy legs, can become very aggressive.

Kori bustards

Another resident bird is the bustard, of which there are 25 species world-wide. Nineteen of these are found in Africa and six in Tanzania. The Kori bustard is the largest flying bird in tropical Africa. Adult males can weigh 18 kg and the colouration of males and females is similar with a flat, brown crown on their heads, grey-white neck and belly and light-brownish feathers covering the back.

Kori bustards will be seen solitary or in pairs walking with long strides across open ground. Courting males puff out their neck feathers and a spine-like section on their backs. They are very photogenic and visible several km away.

There are a number of other notable avian inhabitants of the crater floor. Cape rooks, black and crowlike, noisily caw and burble.

Stately Crowned cranes with large, bare white cheek patches topped with scarlet, slate-grey necks and bodies and straw-coloured, ornamental plumes, perform their courtship "hop-dance" pairing up in the rainy season and forming large flocks in the drier months.

Long-legged black-and-grey-feathered Secretary birds, their distinctive red eye-patches and black quills or plumes drooping behind their necks, stride with measured gait in search of insects, rodents and reptiles which they stamp to death, while ungainly, stout, casque-billed hornbills probe the ground or move ponderously in flight.

Saddle-billed storks

Hornbills in common with many birds are omnivorous, eating both fruit and insects. But the female hornbill's post-mating habits are unique. After mating, in a tree or cliff face, she seals herself into the nest cavity with mud. As incubation begins, the small entry hole is reduced to a slit through which the male feeds his mate. The female moults completely during this period emerging after 25 to 40 days and leaving the chicks to reseal themselves in the nest with excrement.

One bird which seems to be almost everywhere, but especially near the shoreline, is the Blacksmith plover. Its white cap and hind-neck patch, and its black and white plumage, make it readily recognisable. Its voice, like a blacksmith hammering an anvil, is a harsh *klink klink* and it is remarkably brave, attacking anything which goes near its ground-nest while emitting a strident *kewah* sound.

Goose Ponds in the northwest of the crater provides an insight into the diversity of Ngorongoro's colourful waterbirds, although the seasons (wet and dry) determine the avian composition. European migrants such as Swallows, Yellow wagtails and White storks, descend on the area from November coinciding with the rains in the area thereby escaping the European winter. They depart from February to May heading back for the European summer. Other birds, such as the pitta, are intra-African migrants.

Long-legged, mournful-looking Marabou stork are readily identifiable by their long, broad bills and the few tufts of hair on their ugly heads and necks. They are scavengers most often seen around the kills of other animals, waiting in water to seize fish who surface to breath, and around areas of human habitation. In dried-up areas they urinate on their legs to cool them.

Egyption geese, often in large groups, make their raucous voices heard, Grey and Black-headed heron, Hammerkop with the distinctive projection at the back of their heads, white African spoonbills perpetually searching the bottom of ponds with their broad beaks for algae, Yellow-billed duck,

A flock of Lesser flamingo feeding at Ngorongoro's Lake Magadi

Flamingo

Dominant, in both size and numbers, for part of the year at Lake Magadi, are Greater and Lesser flamingo. The Lesser flamingo are a deeper pink with dark-red, black-tipped bills, bright red legs and feet, largely red wings with black flight feathers and yellow eyes. The bill, legs and feet of juveniles are grey and immature birds are whitish with no red on the wings.

Rarely are the two species found occupying the same space but their perpetual humming and movement may make separation difficult. They gather in immense numbers at Rift Valley soda lakes, packing closely together in the water. Lesser flamingo, heads immersed and upside down, feed on minute algae as they wade, while Greater flamingo prefer invertebrates. Mud and water are expelled through their filtered bills with the tongue acting as a piston.

These tall, slender wading birds have long, sinuous necks and thin bills which bend sharply downwards at the midpoint. Their legs are extremely long and they have short webbed toes.

They fly in long skeins or in V-formations, legs and necks fully extended, with their wings audibly beating. The Greater flamingo makes a goose-like honk while the Lesser flamingo makes a high-pitched kwirrik in flight and a softer murr-err on the ground .

Both breed in huge numbers, the Greater flamingo on open shores or small islands, and the Lesser flamingo in dense colonies on open mud. Concentrations of feeding birds can exceed one million at Lakes Nakuru and Bogoria further north.

Hottentot and Red-billed teal, distinguished black and white Sacred ibis and brilliantly coloured, elegant Saddle-billed stork are just a few of the waterbirds in evidence.

Along the shoreline many other birds also feed. Among them are the orange-legged Ruff, Grey-headed gull, Cape wigeon with their grey-pink bills and mottled bodies, kittlitz sandplover, curlew sandpipers, Little stint and Black-winged stilt.

In the wet season, in the Mandusi Swamp just north of Lake Magadi and in the Gorigor swamp to the south of the crater, many smaller, spectacular birds gather. These include Jackson's widow birds who transform themselves from drab, house sparrow colours in the dry season to an unrecognisable long, black tailed and bodied bird with buff shoulders, in the breeding season.

The males' breeding antics include dancing on and flattening a ring of grass, swaying sideways, changing his song to a wheezing, sizzling sound, making a rattling noise with his wings, arching his tail and jumping a metre off the ground with half-open, shivering wings and raised neck feathers. All that effort deserves someone's attention.

Fischer's lovebirds

During the journey around the crater floor, many vultures, probably on the carcass of a kill, will be encountered. Several of the six species may be mixed together, and amidst dry season dust and the disputatious and frenetic action, they are often hard to tell apart. But one will most certainly be the Ruppell's griffon which breeds in Olkarien Gorge in the north of the area.

Eagles also exist in profusion. Three, the Black-chested, Brown and Banded, are snake eagles. One of the most distinctive is the black and white African fish eagle which is usually found in pairs near water where they largely feed on fish as well as waterbirds including flamingo. The mournful, gull-like calls between the pair is another notable sound in the African symphony.

The Lerai Forest provides cover, food and nesting sites for a diverse range of birds. Raucous bulbul and chattering guinea fowl intermingle with many other species including francolin, brilliant yellow weaver, Red-chested cuckoo, warblers, bee-eaters and shrikes. Ascending from Lerai Forest to the crater rim it is difficult not to recognise that Ngorongoro has revealed yet another face.

TREES AND SHRUBS

For those for whom trees and shrubs blur into a sea of green with no discernible meaning or individual identity, their medicinal value to the northern Tanzanian and Kenyan people adds a new and interesting dimension.

These uses cover applications for all manner of ailments ranging from eye disorders, rheumatism, malaria, headaches, acne, common coughs and colds, worms, indigestion, cuts and other wounds, smallpox, sexually transmitted diseases, and there is even one used to treat tortoise bites.

Leonotis mollissima is one of the shrubs most widely used by the Maasai. It is a local common woody herb growing to three metres in height on forest margins, roadsides and disturbed grasslands. Its flowers are red, orange or white and the top of the leaves slightly sandpapery.

An extract from the roots is used for wounds, festering sores and intestinal worms, an infusion is drunk for dysentery and intestinal disorders, leaves and buds used for conjunctivitis, leaves chewed to cure stomach cramps and the plant is also used for indigestion.

Gnarled bark of a yellow fever tree

Several other plants are also used by the Maasai. *Crotalaria agatiflora*, a shrub or tree with pale yellow flowers found beside roads and on the edges of cultivation, is used to treat gonorrhoea as is *Asparagus racemosus*, *Aspilia mossambicensis* and *Cussonia Kirkii*. Some *Cussonia* wood is hollowed to make wild beehives, which you may see hanging in trees, and mole traps.

Several other plants including the roots of *Anthericum suffruticosam*, the chewed leaves of *Bersama Abyssinica*, *Hibiscus aponeurus* and *Stephania Abyssinica* (also used for tortoise bite wounds) are taken as aphrodisiacs.

The Iraqw people cut and boil the thick leaves of *Aloe secundiflora* to treat eye diseases in both people and cattle while the Pare use *Euphorbia Sp.*, which they call *Mkirumbii*, in their extreme treatment of piles and worms with the branches stripped of thorns inserted in the rectum.

Several other plants are used to treat post-natal ailments such as *Aloe spp.* And *Euphorbia candelabrum*, known as *Mkalamu* in Swahili, is used to induce abortions, and for indigestion.

Plants used to treat malaria are *Cassia didymobotrya, Clutia Abyssinica, Hagenia Abyssinica* and *Pentas longiflora.* Other plants are used to treat measles and smallpox while *Hibiscus fuscus* is used as an antidote for any poisoning.

These applications and the dosages are passed down through generations of village healers (traditional medicine people and not "witchdoctors" as they are so frequently called by foreigners) who are greatly respected in their communities for their healing powers and knowledge.

A vervet monkey

Without their advice and expert knowledge it can be highly dangerous, particularly with certain plants, to use these cures without guidance. An overdose of *Cassia didymobotrya* can be fatal while others can easily have unwelcome side-effects.

Beyond their purely medicinal uses, the plants also have functional application. *Vernonia auriculifera* is used to make poultices and medicine containers, *Bersama Abyssinica* as a snuff for colds, *Arundinaria alpina* as bamboo fencing and/or other temporary construction, *Acacia lahai* by the construction industry and the strong, surprisingly pliable timber of

Calodendrum capense, also known as Cape chestnut in English, in house building and to make utilities such as stools and knife handles.

Now equipped with an insight into the added application of trees and shrubs, the visitor is prepared to confront the sea of green they encounter once they enter the conservation area.

What you first see is montane forest. This type of forest, up to some 18000 years ago when the climate was colder, may have extended throughtout the whole region. Now it is only found in isolated mountainous pockets, and it is being encroached upon by fire and Iraqw farmers seeking to expand their cultivation areas.

Beyond the Crater View the vegetation is heavily influenced by the swirling mist. White orchids and moss grow

Old Man's Beard

parasitically on the trees and the grass is green throughout the year. Forest and glade are interspersed with two types of grass, the tussocks of *Eleusine jaegeri* or Makutian grass, and the dense mats of *Cynodon dactylon* or common star grass, competing for space.

During the short rains the area is enlivened by the bright scarlet balls of *Boophane disticha,* commonly known as the Pom-pom flower, and early in the year, the yellow-green blossoms of *Crotalaria imperialis.*

During the rains elephant, buffalo, waterbuck and zebra amidst Maasai livestock, may all be seen in this area while lion, leopard, hyena and bushpig also occur.

FACILITIES

All visitors to the conservation area, whether they have entered via the official Lodoare or Naabi Hill Gates or through an unofficial entry point, must have valid permits which are good for 24-hour periods. Camping fees are also for 24-hour periods and it is advisable to book well in advance to ensure space. Details of camp sites, facilities and fees can be obtained from the Ngorongoro Tourism Office. Night-time cold season temperatures (June-August) can be close to freezing and warm clothing is strongly advised. Sturdy boots, muted environmentally-friendly coloured clothing, sun glasses and a hat are also advised. Binoculars are a strongly suggested supplement while cameras are optional.

The conservation area tourism office is one km from the main road towards the staff village. At this office fees can be paid, permits obtained, vehicles and guides hired, camping details obtained, maps and guide books purchased, radio messages sent and received.

This village is the hub of Ngorongoro's facilities. A post office where you can buy stamps, post mail and make telephone calls, is located near the tourism office. Across the street is the petrol station where you can buy fuel and at the nearby garage assistance is given with vehicle repairs. Some hotels also have repair facilities. Basic goods can be obtained at shops in the village, but if you are not staying in a lodge it is as well to be self-contained. Medical facilities are limited with a small local health clinic. In cases of emergency the Flying Doctor service can be summoned from Nairobi less than an hour away, which can land (if the weather permits) at the Ngorongoro strip.

Only 4x4 vehicles are allowed in the crater and entry will be rationalised, both in terms of the number permitted to enter at a given time and the number of passengers in each vehicle, to prevent over-crowding. For those who have used public or private transport to get to Ngorongoro, 4x4 vehicles are available for hire at the crater. Entry to the conservation area on a motorcycle or bicycle is dangerous and therefore forbidden. However long walks and short hikes can be organised by tour operators. More details can be supplied by the Conservators office.

Most of the hotels admit non-resident customers for meals and drinks and they prepare lunch boxes for residents making a day's outing.

At Ngorongoro there is a choice of six lodges with varying prices and a total bed capacity of 832. Smaller lodges or cottages are located on farms outside the conservation area, and there are 16 special camps at designated sites. There is no student hostel. The international dialing code for Tanzania is 255. Arusha is 57 and Dar es Salaam 51.

Novotel Mount Meru, Arusha

Box 877, Arusha. Tel: 2711/2, 8804, 8737. Fax: 8503, 8925, 8803. On the outskirts of Arusha beside Tanzania's second highest peak, Mount Meru, this hotel is managed by the international ACCOR group. It is three-star with 148 rooms and 20 suites. Its facilities make it Arusha's leading hotel. It has a main restaurant, lobby bar, pool, snack bar, and conference room for 100 delegates. A 30-minute drive from Kilimanjaro Intemational Airport, it is central to Tanzania's famous northern circuit including Ngorongoro, the Serengeti and Kilimanjaro.

Ngorongoro Crater Lodge

Box 751, Arusha. Tel: 8078, 3303. Fax: 8268. This lodge, located on the crater rim, is a Conservation Corporation Africa development on the site of Ngorongoro's oldest hotel. The new Malian-style architecture which encompasses three units of luxurious lodges seems incongruous. The food is good although the facilities are not open to non-residents.

Ngorongoro Rhino Lodge

Box 776, Arusha. Tel: 3339, 4619 Fax: 3339. This lodge, part of the NCAA, is the cheapest at Ngorongoro. It is set back from the crater rim in a secluded patch of forest. The accommodation is clean and simple, food good and the log fire lounge has a warm and cosy atmosphere.

Ngorongoro Serena Safari Lodge

Box 2551, Arusha, Tel: 8175, 6304. Fax: 4058. Designed around the theme of prehistoric life which gave birth to Ngorongoro, and near Olduvai Gorge, this lodge has unhindered views of the crater. It is on a livestock trail to the crater; the tinkle of cow bells are a reminder of Ngorongoro's multiple land-use designation with pastoralists and livestock sharing part of the crater floor.

Ngorongoro Wildlife Lodge

Box 877, Arusha. Tel: 8150, 2404, 2711/2. Fax: 8221. TAHI reservations. Dar es Salaam: Tel & Fax: 116600. Arusha: Tel: 4317. Fax: 8502, 8071. Perched on Ngorongoro's rim, this 75 room lodge offers spectacular views of the crater. It is managed by the international ACCOR group and the hotel is one of a chain (the others being in Serengeti, Manyara and Mafia Island) which belong to the parastatal, Tanzania Hotel Investments (TAHI) which is being privatised.

Sheraton Hotel, Dar es Salaam

Box 791, Dar es Salaam. Tel: 112416. Fax: 113981. The only five-star hotel in the country's commercial capital, next to the golf course and close to the Indian Ocean. Has 250 rooms including suites. The hotel has two restaurants: the Serengeti serving continental food and the Raj serving authentic Indian cuisine. There are two bars, the Kibo and the Pool Bar. Shops selling jewellery, curios, books, pastries as well as a dry cleaners, travel agency, business centre and hair salon are some of the facilities available in the hotel's shopping arcade. Has conference facilities.

Operators

Air Tanzania Corporation

ATC House, Ohio Street, Box 543, Dar es Salaam. Tel: 110245/8, 110273/8. Fax: 113114. Telex: 41253. Flies B737 and F27 aircraft. Destinations: **Middle East:** Dubai, Muscat, Aden and Jeddah; **East-Central Africa:** Kigali, Entebbe, Nairobi, Mombasa, Bujumbura, Kilimanjaro, Zanzibar and Dar es Salaam; **Southern Africa:** Lusaka, Harare, Blantyre, Lilongwe and Johannesburg.

Alliance Air

Box 3053, Arusha. Tel: (0811) 335737/9. Fax: 4444. Box 76404, Dar es Salaam. Tel: 117044/8. Fax: 116715. E-mail Alliance@raha.com. With a B747 SP, leased from South African Airways, Alliance operates direct flights to London-Heathrow, with worldwide connections from Kilimanjaro, Dar es Salaam and Kampala. There are eight sleeperettes in first class, 32 business and 206 economy seats with ample legroom.

Precision Air

Box 1636, Arusha. Tel: 6903, 2818, 7319. Fax: 8204. Telex: 42148/50008.

Mobile: (0811) 888.644. E-mail: precision-ark@cybernet.co.tz. Flies daily: Dar-Zanzibar-Arusha; Mwanza-Bukoba and Seronera-Manyara-Arusha Kilimanjaro-Mombasa. Twice weekly: Dar-Zanzibar-Kilimanjaro-Mwanza; Bukoba-Mwanza-Shinyanga-Arusha; and Mwanza-Ngara. Three times a week: Dar-Shinyanga-Mwanza and its new destinations include Njombe, Mafia and Pemba. Precision also hires charter planes.

Bushbuck Safaris

Box 1700, Arusha. Tel: 7473, 7779, 4186, 8924. Fax: 8293, 2954. Email: bushbuck@yako.habari.co.tz. Bushbuck's experience on the northern circuit minimises the discomfort. Safari prepared 4x4 vehicles are fitted with radios and experienced drivers guide you through Ngorongoro Crater, the Serengeti, Manyara, Arusha and Tarangire national parks. Treks up Kilimanjaro and visits to Zanzibar are catered for.

Kudu Safaris

Box 1404, Arusha. Tel: 8193, 6065. Fax: 8298. E-mail: kudu@habari.co.tz. Specialises in 4x4 lodge and tented camp safaris. With a fleet of specially adapted landcruisers and some of Tanzania's top guides it offers tailor-made safaris and group departures. Safaris are operated to the highest standards at competitive rates. Brochures are supplied of set safaris as well as ideas for a tailor-made "safari of a lifetime".

Roy Safaris

Box 50, Arusha. Tel: 2115, 8010, 7057. Fax: 8892. Email: roysafaris@habari.co.tz Web address: http://www.intafrica.com./roysafaris. Operates 23 vehicles with 24 guides/drivers and 22 camp crew. Speciality lodge and camping safaris to all parks including Serengeti, Ngorongoro, Manyara and Tarangire. Treks up Mount Kilimanjaro and Mount Meru and tours to Zanzibar among tailor-made safaris.

Wildersun Safaris

Box 2587, Arusha. Tel: 8847/9, 3880, 2491, 3571. Fax: 8223. E-mail: wildersun@habari.co.tz. The name embraces wildlife and sunshine and the logo says they are the "in" people to go "out" with. Established in 1980 by husband and wife team Merwyn and Pervin Nunes, who have over 50 years' experience in the travel industry. Experienced guides undertake exclusive wildlife viewing and photographic safaris.

CHECKLIST

MAMMALS

Primates
Greater galago (bushbaby)
Lesser galago (bushbaby)
Olive baboon
Vervet monkey
Blue (Sykes) monkey
Pholidota
Ground pangolin
Lagomorpha
Hare
Rodentia
Porcupine
Tree squirrel
Bush squirrel
Spring hare
Carnivora
Golden jackal
Side-striped jackal
Black-backed jackal
African hunting dog
Bat-eared fox
Polecat
Honey badger
Spot-necked otter
Clawless otter
Small-spotted genet
Large-spotted genet
Civet
Greater-grey mongoose
Lesser mongoose
Dwarf mongoose
Marsh mongoose
Banded mongoose
White-tailed mongoose
Aardwolf
Spotted hyena
Striped hyena
Wild cat
Caracal

Serval cat
Leopard
Lion
Cheetah
Tubulidentata
Aardvark
Proboscidea
Elephant
Hyracoidea
Rock hyrax
Tree hyrax
Perissodactyla
Burchell's zebra
Black rhinoceros
Artiodactyla
Bushpig
Warthog
Hippopotamus
Giraffe
Lesser kudu
Bushbuck
Eland
Buffalo
Red duiker
Bush duiker
Waterbuck
Bohor reedbuck
Mountain reedbuck
Oryx
Coke's hartebeest (Kongoni)
Wildebeest
Klipspringer
Oribi
Steinbok
Dikdik
Impala
Thomson's gazelle
Grant's gazelle
Suni

FURTHER READING

INTO AFRICA TRAVEL GUIDES

TANZANIA
Serengeti: Endless Plains
Ngorongoro: Book of Life
*Kilimanjaro: African Beacon**
*Zanzibar: Spice Islands**
*The Northern Circuit**
*The Southern Circuit**
*The Tanzanian Coast**

ZIMBABWE
Great Zimbabwe: Houses of Stone
Victoria Falls: Mosi-oa-Tunya
Kariba: Nyaminyami's Kingdom
Hwange: Elephant Country
Bvumba: Magic in the Mist
*Harare: Sunshine City**
*Bulawayo: Home of Kings**
*Nyanga: A Touch of Europe**
*Chimanimani: Hikers Paradise**

OTHER AFRICAN PUBLISHING GROUP TITLES
Dawn to Dusk: A Safari Through Africa's Wild Places, Jonathan Scott
Great Zimbabwe Described and Explained, Peter Garlake
The Hunters Vision: The Prehistoric Art of Zimbabwe, Peter Garlake
The Smoke That Thunders, Dusty Durrant
The Soapstone Birds of Great Zimbabwe, Edward Matenga
Rhodes, Antony Thomas
A Political History of Munhumutapa: c 1400-1902, Dr Stan Mudenge

OTHER NGORONGORO READING
Ngorongoro's First Visitor
Ngorongoro's Geological History
Ngorongoro's Bird Life
Ngorongoro's Animal Life
Ngorongoro's Trees and Shrubs
Ngorongoro: The Eighth Wonder, Henry Fosbrooke (Andre Deutsch)
Olduvai Gorge: My Search for Early Man, Mary Leakey (Collins)
Multiple Land-Use: The Experience of Ngorongoro (IUCN)
Ngorongoro, Reinhard Kunkel (Harper Collins)
Maasai, Tepilit Ole Saitoti and Carol Beckwith (Harper Collins)
Pastoral Man in the Garden of Eden, Kaj Arhem (Uppsala)
Ngorongoro Conservation Area Handbook, Jeanette Hanby and D

* forthcoming

INDEX